From the Workshop to the Boardroom

THE POWER OF YES AND… COMMUNICATION

Jaime Rich and Randy Wight

i/Me
PUBLISHING GROUP
INSPIRE-MOTIVATE-EMPOWER

Jaime Rich, Randy Wight

Copyright © 2024 IME Publishing Group

ALL RIGHTS RESERVED no part of this book, or its associated ancillary materials may be re- produced or transmitted in any form or by any means, electronic or mechanical, including photocopying, recording, or by any information of storage or retrieval system without the per- mission from the publisher.

PUBLISHED BY IME

Publishing Group DISCLAIMER

AND/OR LEGAL NOTICES

While all attempts have been made to verify the information provided in this book and its ancillary materials, neither the author or the publisher assume any responsibility for errors, inaccuracies or omissions and is not responsible for any financial loss by consumer in any manner. Any slights of people or organizations are unintentional. If advice concerning legal, financial, accounting or related matters is needed, the service of a qualified professional should be sought. This book and its associated axillary materials, including verbal and written training, is not intended for use as a source of legal, financial or accounting advice. You should be aware of the various laws governing business transactions or other business practices in your particular geographical location.

EARNINGS AND INCOME DISCLAIMER

With respect to the reliability, accuracy, timeliness, usefulness, adequacy, completeness, and/or suitability of information provided in the book, Jaime Rich, Randy Wight, and IME Publishing Group its Partners Associates Affiliates Consultants and/or presenters make no warranties guarantees representations or claims of any kind. Readers' results will vary depending on a number of factors. Any and all claims or representations as to income earnings are not to be considered and average earnings. Testimonials are not representative. This book and all products and services are for education and informational purposes only. Use caution and see the advice of qualified professionals. Check with your accountant, attorney or professional adviser before acting on this or any information. You agreed that Jaime Rich, Randy Wight, and IME Publishing Group is not responsible for the success or failure of your personal, business, health or financial decisions relating to any information presented by Jaime Rich, Randy Wight, and IME Publishing Group or Company products/ services. Earnings potentials is entirely dependent on the efforts, skills and application of the individual person. Exercises and ideas in the information materials offered are simply opinion or experience, and thus should not be misinterpreted as promises, typical results or guarantees (expressed or implied). The author and the publisher Jaime Rich, Randy Wight, ME Publishing Group (IME or any IME

From the Workshop to the Boardroom

Representatives) Shall in no way, under any circumstances be held liable to any party (or third-party) for any direct, indirect, punitive, special, incidental or other consequential damages arising directly or indirectly from any use of books, materials and or seminar trainings, which is provided "as is," and without warranties Jaime Rich, Randy Wight/ IME Publishing Group.

Any examples, stories, references, or case studies are for illustrative purposes only and should not be interpreted as testimonies and/or examples of what reader and/ or consumers are generally expected from the information. No representation in any part of this information, materials and/ or seminar trainings are guarantees or promises for actual performance. Any statements, strategies, concepts, techniques, exercises and ideas in the information materials and/or seminar training offered are simply opinion or experience, and thus should not be misinterpreted as promises, typical results or guarantees (expressed or implied). The author and the publisher (Jaime Rich, Randy Wight, IME Publishing Group, IME or any IME Representatives) Shall in no way, under any circumstances be held liable to any party (or third-party) for any direct, indirect, punitive, special, incidental or other consequential damages arising directly or indirectly from any use of books, materials and or seminar trainings, which is provided "as is," and without warranties Jaime Rich, Randy Wight/IME Publishing Group.

IME Publishing Group
1990 N California Blvd. Suite 20 PMB 1065
Walnut Creek, California 94596

1-866-726-6563
www.IMEPublishingGroup.com
Jaime Rich, Randy Wight,-1st ed.

Jaime Rich, Randy Wight

The Power of Yes And...Communication Companion Workbook.

Download this concise companion workbook for supplemental information, examples, and exercises. This workbook goes hand in hand with the Yes And...Communication book that Jaime and Randy have created. Short summaries are provided on topics such as The Constant Flow of Change, Make Your Partner Look Good, Spontaneity and more!

bit.ly/yesandworkbook

Contents

Foreword 1

The Constant Flow of Change: Navigating Uncertainty and Embracing Innovation 9

The Constant Flow of Change 17

Getting Comfortable with Discomfort 29

Spontaneity–The Confidence to Speak What First Comes to Your Mind 39

Making Your Partner Look Good 49

There Are No Mistakes–The Benefits of Embracing Failure 61

The Importance of the Psychological Safety of Improv 71

Improv and the Meta View or Outside View of Self .. 83

Channeling Childlike Essence 95

Laughter! 107

About the Authors 117

Jaime Rich, Randy Wight

From the Workshop to the Boardroom

Foreword

"Yes, and...means agreeing to the reality that your partner is setting for you."

Jaime Rich/Randy Wight

In a world where uncertainty often leads us to say *no*, Jaime Rich and Randy Wight, renowned experts in the realm of improvisational theater, unfold the trans-formative potential of a simple yet powerful word: *Yes*. Their book, *The Power of Yes and Communication*, is not just a testament to the art of improvisation but a guide to embracing positivity and connectivity in every aspect of life.

Jaime Rich, Randy Wight

"Communication is a skill that you can learn. It's like riding a bicycle or typing. If you're willing to work at it, you can rapidly improve the quality of every part of your life."

Brian Tracy

At the core of improvisational theater lies the principle of acceptance, epitomized by the phrase "Yes, and..." This concept encourages actors to accept whatever their fellow performers introduce and then to add to it, building a narrative collaboratively and spontaneously. The performers need to accept the reality that their partner has set forth for them. Rich and Wight adeptly translate this principle into a life philosophy. This transcends to personal relationships, business relationships, and all areas of life. It is not just for characters on a stage. In explaining this philosophy for life, they offer readers a unique lens through which to view communication, relationships, and personal growth.

The book is a journey through various aspects of life where saying *Yes* can make a profound difference. From personal relationships to professional environments, the authors illustrate how embracing opportunities, new ideas, and different perspectives can lead to growth, innovation, and deeper connections. They combine their extensive experience in improvisation with research in psychology, communication, and business, offering insights that are both practical and profound.

One of the most compelling aspects of *The Power of Yes and Communication* is the ease with which it is written and the ease with which it can be comprehended. Rich and Wight's writing is infused with the same energy and spontaneity found in their improv performances, making complex ideas engaging and easy to understand. They use real-world examples, personal anecdotes, and exercises that readers can apply in their daily lives. This approach not only demystifies the concepts, but also encourages active participation and experimentation.

The book also addresses the challenges and limitations of saying *yes*. The authors recognize it is not a panacea for all life's problems. One cannot always agree to everything that life and people inherent in their life throw at them. Instead, they present it as a starting point for dialogue, creativity, and problem-solving. They discuss how to balance affirmation with critical thinking, how to recognize when to say *no*, and how to use affirmative language to build rather than to acquiesce blindly.

Rich and Wight's expertise in improvisation shines through in their approach to communication. They stress the importance of active listening, empathy, and adaptability. By treating conversations as collaborative improvisations, where each participant contributes and builds upon the others' ideas, they demonstrate how we can create more meaningful and productive interactions.

These partners in crime have created a guide that is as entertaining as it is enlightening, as practical as it is inspiring. It is a must-read for anyone looking to improve their communication skills, build stronger relationships, and lead a more fulfilling life.

From the Workshop to the Boardroom

As you turn these pages, you will be invited not just to read but to act. To say *yes* to new ideas, to open yourself up to new possibilities, and to begin a journey of transformation. Whether you are an improv enthusiast, a professional looking to enhance your communication skills, or someone seeking personal growth, this book holds valuable lessons for you. Embrace the power of *yes*, and watch as the world opens up in ways you never imagined.

> "You must take personal responsibility. You cannot change the circumstances, the seasons, or the wind, but you can change yourself. That is something you have charge of."
>
> — *Jim Rohn*

From the Workshop to the Boardroom

Try This:

Yes, And... This is one of the fundamental principles of improv. In working with your partner, you agree to the reality that they are setting forth for you and then adding on and building from there.

Everyone begins in a circle. Someone will start and say a statement to their partner to the left or right of them in the circle. Their partner will then *yes and* their statement. They will start every reply with, "Yes and..." The play then continues around the circle with new statements and replies. For example, a player may say to their partner, "It's a beautiful day." The partner could reply with, "Yes and, I'm looking forward to going to the beach with you today, Mom."

Jaime Rich, Randy Wight

Chapter 1

NAVIGATING UNCERTAINTY AND EMBRACING INNOVATION

The concept of change is likened to the ebbs and flows of the ocean, highlighting its rhythmic yet unpredictable nature. This comprehensive view is essential for understanding how to adapt and thrive in both personal and professional realms. A pivotal tool in navigating this landscape is applied improvisation. This approach not only helps in understanding the dynamics of change but also equips individuals and organizations with practical skills to manage it effectively.

Understanding Change through Rich and Wight's Lens

They begin by acknowledging the inevitability of change, stressing its continuous presence in our lives. They categorize change into two categories: evolutionary, akin to the steady ebb and flow of tides, and revolutionary, which is sudden and impactful like a tsunami. Understanding these types of change is crucial for developing appropriate strategies.

Applied Improvisation: A Tool for Adaptation and Communication

Central to the discussion is the role of applied improvisation in navigating change. This method, drawn from the principles of theatrical improvisation, emphasizes adaptability, quick thinking, and effective communication. It's useful in responding to unforeseen challenges and in fostering a culture of flexibility and resilience.

Communication and Leadership in Times of Change

Effective communication is vital during times of change. Rich and Wight advocate for the use of applied improvisation to enhance communication skills, enabling individuals to articulate their thoughts clearly and listen actively. This is especially important for leaders who must guide their teams through the uncertainties of change with confidence and clarity.

Emotional Intelligence and Cultural Resilience

They also highlight the emotional aspects of change, noting that applied improvisation can help in managing these responses by fostering emotional intelligence. In an organizational context, this approach contributes to building a culture that is resilient to change, valuing creativity and adaptability.

Innovation and Opportunity in Change

Change, while challenging, presents opportunities for growth and innovation. The theory is that applied improvisation encourages a proactive stance towards change, promoting innovative thinking and the exploration of new possibilities.

Sustainability and Ethical Considerations

Incorporating ethical and sustainable considerations into responses to change is another aspect that should be emphasized. Applied improvisation, with its focus on empathy and collective well-being, guides decision-making to ensure responses are both sustainable and ethically sound.

Preparing for Future Changes

As the future promises an acceleration in the pace and complexity of change, Rich and Wight believe that skills in applied improvisation will become increasingly crucial. The ability to adapt quickly and effectively, maintaining open and effective communication, will be key to navigating future challenges.

Try This:

I Am A Tree. Another element of improv involves creating an environment for the scene. There usually are no sets, no props, etc. The environment exists in the actor's mind and they have to paint the picture for their audience. In this game, they are creating an environment that a player may enter and be part of. This is a three person at a time game. The leader always starts with "*I Am A Tree.*"

One person enters the center of the circle and states, "I am a tree." Then one by one people add on to the environment of a tree. One person might enter and say, "I am a bird." another person might come in and say, "I am a branch." The first person in then decides who they want to take out with them. They may say, "I'm going to take the branch," and then the branch comes out with them. The person left is the bird.

They start a brand-new threesome and a new scene by first restating, "I am a bird." Two people come in one by one to add to that brand new scene-having nothing to do with the prior scene.

In this game, the second person is the person who is deciding which way the scene is going. For example, if in the first scene example with the tree, the branch is left to start the second scene. Branch can mean different things to different people. The second person can come in and say, "I'm Bank of America." It's suddenly not a branch of a tree anymore. It's the branch of a business. The third person would need to enter and say another kind of branch of a business (such as Wells Fargo). The three elements of the scene all need to go together.

Chapter 1 Take Away

Jaime Rich and Randy Wight's exploration of change through the analogy of ocean tides provides a profound understanding of its nature. By emphasizing the role of applied improvisation, they offer a practical tool for navigating the unpredictable waters of change. This approach enhances communication, fosters flexibility, prepares for unpredictability, and supports innovative and sustainable decision-making. Embracing these practices allows individuals and organizations to not just withstand but thrive amidst the constant flux of change.

"Improv doesn't emphasize tension between two people, but they can be facing a challenge and external conflict together."

Jaime Rich/Randy Wight

Chapter 2

The Constant Flow of Change

"Be Curious...."

Tim Orr

Understanding the Nature of Change: The Ebbs and Flows

Change is inevitable in all parts of life-business, personal, etc. It is always prevalent in the business setting, and it is something that we need to wrap our heads around. It is the universal constant upon which the fabric of our existence and the marketplace is woven. Stagnation, the absence of change, is nothing to strive for. Stagnation builds passivity. An acceptance of what is always and what is expected. The nature of change is cyclical, with its ebbs and flows mirroring the natural rhythms of the world. This dynamic movement can bring about growth and innovation, but also uncertainty and resistance. Inherent in the principles of improv is an ability to ride the wave of change. It prepares you to deal with what comes as it comes without planning ahead.

Practicing improv helps one to embrace the positive aspects of change and navigate successfully through the negative aspects.

The Impact of Change on Individuals and Organizations

Change has a multifaceted impact on both individuals and organizations, harboring the potential for positive development and the inherent risk of possible negative outcomes.

Positive Aspects

- Innovation and Creativity: Change forces individuals and organizations out of their comfort zones, leading to innovative thinking and creative problem-solving.
- Growth and Development: It provides opportunities for personal and organizational growth, pushing boundaries and expanding limits.
- Resilience Building: Navigating through change strengthens adaptability and resilience, essential qualities for thriving in today's fast-paced world.

Negative Aspects

- Resistance and Fear: Change often meets resistance, stemming from fear of the unknown and loss of control.

- Stress and Anxiety: It can induce stress and anxiety, impacting well-being and productivity.
- Disruption and Chaos: Without effective management, change can lead to disruption and organizational chaos.

Applied Improvisation as a Mitigative Tool

Applied improvisation, drawing from the principles of improvisational theater, offers tools to navigate the turbulent waters of change. By embracing the improvisational mindset, individuals and organizations can mitigate the negative effects of change.

Techniques for Managing Uncertainty and Anxiety

- *Yes, And...*Thinking: This foundational improv principle encourages acceptance and building upon ideas, fostering a positive and open environment for navigating change.
- Embracing Failure: Improv teaches that failure is not a setback but a step forward, an opportunity for learning and growth. We say in improv that 'there are no mistakes'. We often applaud when someone messes up.

- Flexibility and Adaptability: Practicing improv helps develop the ability to adapt swiftly to changing circumstances and think on one's feet.

The Role of Adaptability and Flexibility

The degree of adaptability and flexibility within an individual or organization significantly influences the outcome of change. A lack of these qualities can lead to poor outcomes and exacerbate the chaos that change might bring. Conversely, high adaptability and flexibility can smooth the transition, turning potential challenges into opportunities.

One principle of improv-Be Spontaneous-can help one be comfortable with not pre-planning but going with a first creative thought. Not harnessing ideas or waiting for the perfect one.

Navigating Uncertainty:
Lessons from the Covid Crisis and Elections

Recent global events, such as the Covid-19 pandemic and various elections, have underscored the importance of navigating through uncertain times. These events have shown that staying grounded and focused, while embracing adaptability and flexibility, can guide us through the most tumultuous periods.

Strategies for Staying Grounded

- Mindfulness and Presence: Staying present and mindful can help maintain focus and reduce anxiety. When one is in an improv scene, for example, and is not present-not accepting of ideas that their partner throws at them-the scene can fall flat. Neither partner feeling satisfied or supported.
- Clear Communication: Effective communication within teams can provide stability and clarity amidst confusion. In improv, we use the terms 'send and receive'. Each partner must be able to send a message successfully (eye contact is key) and receive a message in the same manner. If either of these is not done adequately, neither partner will feel supported or secure.
- One's Community and Support: Leaning on community and building support networks can bolster resilience. In improv (which can transcend into any environment), our partner is our support and we rely on them.

Addressing Resistance to Change with Applied Improvisation

Resistance to change is a natural response but can be managed through applied improvisation techniques.

Strategies Include

- Active Listening: Improv exercises that focus on listening can help address and understand the concerns leading to resistance.
- Role-Playing: Using role-play to simulate changes can help individuals and teams visualize and prepare for the impact, reducing fear and resistance.
- Incremental Changes: Applying the principle of small, incremental changes can ease the transition, making the process less daunting. Progress takes time and patience.

Embracing a Growth Mindset

The concept of a growth mindset, the belief in the capacity to grow and learn, is crucial in embracing change. Applied improvisation, with its focus on continuous learning and adaptability, embodies this mindset. It teaches that discomfort is not an obstacle, but a pathway to growth.

Effective Communication of Change

Communicating change effectively is paramount to the acceptance and success the change can bring. The principles of clarity, empathy, and engagement, drawn from applied improvisation, can significantly enhance this process.

- Clarity and Simplicity: Communicate changes in a clear, straightforward manner.
- Empathy: Understand and acknowledge the feelings and concerns of your audience.
- Engagement: Involve stakeholders and team members in the process, making them active participants in the change. In improv, our stakeholders are first our fellow improvisers and then our theater audience members.

By integrating applied improvisation techniques and embracing a growth mindset, individuals and organizations can navigate the constant flow of change more effectively. This approach not only mitigates the negative impacts of change but also leverages its positive aspects, leading to innovation, growth, and resilience.

Try This:

Count to 20. This is a great way to unite a group. Everyone will stand in a circle. The group needs to collectively count to 20, one number at a time. Anyone can start and the play continues. If two people say a number at the same time, the group needs to start over from one. There should be no admonitions or groaning if this happens. The group simply knows that they will start over. When the group gets to 20, it's a cause to celebrate.

"If a partner brings negativity to a scene or situation, it is up to you to bring them out of it."

Jaime Rich/Randy Wight

What else should I be reading?

What are the best improv books out there? Jaime and Randy have reviewed dozens of books and have produced their top 5. Watch this video to find out why they have picked the ones that they have chosen. They will provide peer reviews of these top 5 and tell you what they have gleaned from each book.

bit.ly/YouShouldBeReading

Chapter 3

Getting Comfortable with Discomfort

Embracing the Unfamiliar: The Path to Growth

There is no planning or preparing for what may happen in improv. This may result in discomfort for those embarking on the improv journey. In this chapter, we delve into discomfort and how embracing this discomfort and working through it can lead to growth and positive change.

The Nature of Discomfort:
A Necessary Unease

Discomfort can be a scary thing and a feeling that most people will avoid. It is mostly viewed as a negative sensation. One that people want to get through as quickly as possible. Ironically, discomfort is inherent in the path to overcoming challenges and becoming stronger in the process.

In improv theater, discomfort is the space between the known script and the uncharted territory of spontaneous creation. It is here, in this gap, where the magic of growth occurs. The magic is in the freedom to create and make up any scenario that one wants. The players are not bound by scripts or words on a page. It is all up to their own imagination and what is in their head. Magic and…scary.

Comfort Zones:
Safe Havens or Prisons?

We all have our comfort zones, those familiar routines, and behaviors where we feel safe and in control. However, Jaime and Randy believe that comfort zones, while reassuring, are often barriers to innovation and growth. In the context of a corporate team, lingering in the comfort zone equates to stagnation. Embracing discomfort means stepping out of these zones and daring to explore new possibilities. There is an entire world out there-out of our own personal comfort zones.

Distinguishing Healthy Discomfort from Unhealthy Stress

Not all forms of discomfort are beneficial. It's crucial to distinguish between the discomfort that fosters growth and the stress that depletes. Healthy discomfort feels like a stretch, a challenge that is invigorating and exciting. Unhealthy stress, on the other hand, feels draining and overwhelming. The key is to recognize and navigate these differences effectively. When Jaime teaches a class or works with a team in a corporate environment, she strives to constantly check the discomfort temperature of the group. If the group are rolling their eyes or visibly stressed by the activity, she will move on to another one.

Techniques for Embracing Discomfort

The art of improv offers a treasure trove of techniques for embracing discomfort.

These include:

- Yes, And…: Accepting what is offered and building upon it, rather than resisting or negating new ideas.
- Active Listening: Truly hearing and adapting to the contributions of others, an essential skill in both improv and collaborative environments.
- Adaptability: Being flexible and open to change, an invaluable trait in the face of uncertainty. In improv, we teach each partner must be open to whatever their partner lays forth for them. They need to be able to be changed by what their partner endows them with.

Building Resilience and Perseverance

Resilience is the ability to bounce back from adversity and discomfort. Improv gives one the tools to persevere through this discomfort. These two principles-resiliency and perseverance involve developing a tolerance for uncertainty and a determination to persist despite setbacks. In improv, every misstep is an opportunity for learning, a principle that translates seamlessly into the corporate world.

Managing Fear and Limiting Beliefs

Fear can hold us back and keep us in our comfort zones. In addition, if we don't believe in ourselves and our abilities, it is difficult to move forward and to grow. Jaime and Randy emphasize the importance of techniques such as mindfulness and cognitive restructuring to manage these impediments. Recognizing and challenging one's limiting beliefs paves the way for embracing new, growth-oriented mindsets.

The Role of Self-Talk:
Angel vs. Devil

The internal dialogue, often a battle between the encouraging *Angel* and the discouraging *Devil*, plays a crucial role in how we approach discomfort. Positive self-talk, an integral aspect of improv training, helps in reframing perspectives and overcoming fear. We learn to shoo away the devil and concentrate on the words of the encouraging angel who believes in us and our abilities to thrive.

Reframing Negative Thoughts and Beliefs

Reframing involves altering our perception of a situation. By changing our narrative and our self-talk, we can transform challenges into opportunities and discomfort into a learning experience. Some questions to ask ourselves in the face of negative self-talk:

- What is the evidence of this?
- Has this negative result happened in the past?
- Are there positives that can come from us taking this on?

From the Workshop to the Boardroom

Cultivating a Support System

No one embraces discomfort in isolation. A support system, akin to an improv troupe, provides the encouragement and perspective needed to venture beyond the comfort zone. In a corporate setting, this translates to a culture of mutual support and open communication. If we have people in our corner, people who we can trust and turn to, it makes it much easier to push through and strive. We should count on these people to be our *angels*, to at least provide positive messaging and turn around our negative thoughts.

Try This:

Anybody Else. It's a great way to start a group going and to find commonalities within the group, to get people to know each other. And it's a lot of fun too! One person is going to start by saying something that is true for them. It can be anything, something they like, where they grew up, brothers and sisters, cats, and dogs, etc. Whatever. Something that's true for them. Then everyone else, which that is true for, walks toward that first person. Then someone else in the group will say something that's true for them and people will walk towards them. There is no order. Anyone can shout out something that's true for them and people move around the room.

Take Aways:

The Improviser's Journey

The journey to getting comfortable with discomfort is continuous and evolving. Like an improviser on stage, we are constantly adapting, learning, and growing. By embracing the principles discussed in this chapter, individuals and teams can transform discomfort from a source of anxiety into a wellspring of innovation and personal growth.

"Get out of your comfort zone and know that your thoughts will be met without judgement or negativity"

Randy Wight/Jaime Rich

Jaime Rich, Randy Wight

Chapter 4

SPONTANEITY–THE CONFIDENCE TO SPEAK WHAT FIRST COMES TO YOUR MIND

> "Say whatever comes to your mind-just spit it out"

Jaime Rich/Randy Wight

From the Workshop to the Boardroom

In the bustling world of corporate teams, where innovation and efficiency are paramount, the intro-duction of spontaneity can often seem like a crazy and scary notion. Yet, it is precisely this element that Jaime Rich and Randy Wight, seasoned improv producers, directors, and performers, champion in their trans-formative approach. Spontaneity, as explored in this chapter, is not merely about being unpredictable; it's about harnessing the power of the moment to foster creativity, enhance communication, and build a resilient and adaptive work culture.

The Essence of Spontaneity

At its core, spontaneity is the fuel for creativity and innovation. It encourages individuals to think on their feet, stepping out of the confines of over-analysis and into the realm of immediate action. Pre-thinking and planning are counterintuitive when it comes to improv. We teach people to get out of their heads, to spit out the first idea that comes to them. This is often uncomfortable. Will my ideas be met with resistance? Will they be embraced? Building on the yes and...culture of improv, we learn our ideas will be agreed to and added on to by our partners.

When we become comfortable with this notion, it is easier to trust ourselves to say the first thing that comes into our minds. This shift from deliberation to action allows for a free flow of ideas, unhampered by the self-censorship that often stifles creativity. Jaime's mantra, "Don't waste time thinking about it—just spit it out!" encapsulates this ethos, urging us to let ideas flow freely, making room for collaboration and expansion by others.

Spontaneity in Communication

Effective communication thrives on spontaneity. The ability to *spit it out*—to convey thoughts and ideas without overthinking—can lead to more authentic and dynamic exchanges. We encourage people not to strive to be the cleverest, the most creative, etc. This requires thought and deliberation. On the other hand, the immediacy that comes with spontaneity fosters an environment where team members feel valued and heard, as spontaneous dialogue often reveals underlying truths and insights that premeditated communication may overlook.

Cultivating a Spontaneous Work Culture

Incorporating spontaneity into the fabric of work culture can significantly benefit an organization. It encourages a mindset of flexibility and openness, essential components in navigating the ever-changing corporate landscape. Spontaneity in the workplace leads to active listening, as team members become more attuned to responding to and building on others' ideas, fostering a collaborative atmosphere that can pivot and adapt as challenges arise. It, in turn, builds a collective and trusting group of people who feel free to share ideas without judgement or ridicule.

Techniques for Being Present and Responsive

To harness the benefits of spontaneity, it is crucial to develop techniques for staying present and responsive. Exercises such as *One Word Story*, where each participant adds a word to build a story, has a group working together to create a finished product of a story. We also do an exercise called *Three Things* where one partner asks another for three things that answer a prompt such as; three things under your bed, three things you wear on your head, etc. There are no wrong answers. The goal is to spit out three things without pause that at least somewhat answer the prompt. More important, though, is to say the first three things that come to one's mind. The entire group then acknowledges them by saying, "Three Things!" together.

Building Rapport and Trust Through Spontaneity

Spontaneity plays a vital role in building rapport and trust within teams. It signals a willingness to be vulnerable and open, traits that are foundational to strong, trusting relationships. By engaging in spontaneous dialogue and activities, team members can break down barriers and foster a sense of unity and mutual respect. People end up feeling more comfortable to share their ideas with ease and without hesitation.

Leveraging Humor and Storytelling

Humor and storytelling are powerful tools in enhancing communication, and spontaneity amplifies their impact. Through improvisational exercises like the ones Jaime prefers, teams learn to use humor and narrative to connect and convey messages in engaging and memorable ways. An easy spontaneity game to try is to go through any category of things alphabetically in a group one by one. For instance, types of cars, girl's names, ice cream flavors. The participants are encouraged to spit out anything that starts with that letter (even nonsense words) if they can't come up with something.

Role Play and Responding to Challenges

Improv-based role play scenarios provide a safe space for individuals to practice responding to unexpected challenges. This training ground for spontaneity equips team members with the confidence and skill to navigate real-world situations with agility and composure. These will look different depending on the business and the environment. As close to real-life situations as possible, works the best to equip the team members to deal successfully when situations arise.

Overcoming Resistance

While spontaneity offers numerous benefits, it's common to encounter resistance, especially from those who prefer planning and predictability. Overcoming this resistance involves demonstrating the value of spontaneity in generating new ideas and solutions, and fostering an environment where all team members feel supported in stepping out of their comfort zones. The best way to navigate this is to start slow, with small steps, simple exercises like the ones in this chapter. People will hopefully learn that they don't always have to plan, but that spontaneity can only enhance and add to their toolbox.

Try This:

Three things. It's a tried-and-true improv exercise. It works on one of the three principles of improv, which is spontaneity. To be comfortable and be able to spit out anything and know that it will be received warmly and without judgment. The key to this game is to not think, not get in your head, but just to blurt out the answers. The group should get in a circle. Our partners, in this case, are going to be the people on either side of us. You will ask your partner for three things that fall into some category.

Such as *three things you wear on your head, three things under your bed, three things that you would say to your dog*, etc. The goal is to blurt out those three things in answer to your partner as quickly as you can and without thinking. The answers do not have to be correct, clever, or perfect. They also shouldn't be in reality (for instance, three things that are really under your bed). If they can fall under the category that your partner is given to you, great. But the main thing is just to get out those words. Then we're all going to say, "Three Things!" which is a good way of really saying good job.

Take Away

Spontaneity, as Jaime Rich and Randy Wight articulate, is more than an improvisational technique; it is a strategic tool that can revolutionize how corporate teams collaborate, innovate, and communicate. By embracing spontaneity, organizations can create a culture of openness and flexibility, ready to meet the challenges of the modern business world with creativity and resilience. Just *Spit it Out'*

> *"Get out of your head, into your space and await the invisible stranger"*
>
> — *Viola Spolin*

Chapter 5

Making Your Partner Look Good

> *"Your partner is the most important person to you on that stage."*
>
> — *Randy Wight/Jaime Rich*

In the world of improv, one of the fundamental principles that drives successful collaboration is the ethos of making your partner look good. If your partner doesn't look good, you don't look good. Improv is almost never a one man show. Your partners are all important to your success. Jaime Rich and Randy Wight, with their extensive background in improv, have brought this principle into the corporate realm to foster environments where collab-oration, trust, and mutual support are at the forefront of team dynamics. This chapter delves into how this principle enhances collaboration, the importance of support and trust, and practical techniques to implement this ethos in a corporate setting.

Enhancing Collaboration through Mutual Support

Making your partner look good first and foremost can lead to success. It isn't just about public praise; it's a philosophy that, when practiced, enhances team collaboration significantly. By focusing on elevating your colleagues, you create a positive feedback loop where everyone feels valued and motivated to contribute their best. This approach shifts the focus from individual achievement to collective success, leading to a more cohesive and productive team environment.

The Role of Support and Trust

Trust and support are the bedrock of successful collaboration. When team members actively work to make their partners look good, it sends a powerful message of trust. It shows that you believe in your partner's abilities and value their contributions. This mutual respect and support naturally lead to a stronger foundation of trust within the team, making collaboration more effective and seamless. In improv, we hope for partners that will always be there for us, and will cover for us when we mess up or make a mistake on stage. It's this confidence in the other person on the stage with us that leads to successful stage and scene work.

Acknowledging and Valuing Contributions

A key aspect of making your partner look good is the acknowledgment and appreciation of their contributions. Recognizing the efforts and inputs of team members not only boosts morale but also fosters a culture of appreciation that strengthens team bonds. Techniques for acknowledging contributions include:

- Publicly crediting ideas and contributions to their originators during meetings.

- Highlighting the successes of team members in team communications or company-wide platforms.
- Encouraging a culture of peer recognition where team members regularly acknowledge and appreciate each other's contributions.
- Practicing and giving validations to our teammates that are specific. More than *good work* or *good job*, try to be specific about what their contribution was. e.g. "I appreciated the artwork that you added on page 4 and 5."

Constructive Feedback and Positive Language

Providing constructive feedback is essential for growth and improvement, but the way it's delivered can make all the difference. Beginning feedback with positive language (taking us back to *Yes and...*) sets a supportive tone and opens the pathway for a constructive conversation. For instance, using phrases like, "I really appreciate the way you handled that situation, and I wonder if we might explore another approach for even greater impact," invites collaboration rather than defensiveness. Starting with *Yes And...* instead of *No But...* or even *Yes But...*

Emphasizing Contributions with Positive Language

Using positive language to emphasize contributions involves more than just praising outcomes; it's about recognizing effort, creativity, and the willingness to take risks. Phrases like, "Your approach really brought a new perspective" or "Your dedication to getting this right is what made the difference," make the receiver feel valued. Again, as specific as you can be in your contributions helps people know exactly what you appreciated.

Acknowledging Expertise and Skills

Beyond general affirmations, acknowledging the specific expertise and skills of team members can empower them and reinforce their value to the team. This can be as simple as saying, "Your expertise in [specific area] was crucial in navigating the challenges we faced," which not only boosts the individual's confidence but also encourages them to continue contributing their unique skills. Ideally, your team is made up of members who bring differing and varied skills to the table.

Supporting Decision-Making

Making your partner look good extends to supporting their decision-making. This support can manifest as backing their proposals in meetings, supporting their ideas to fruition, or simply expressing confidence in their judgment. Sharing ownership and accountability for decisions reinforces the message that *we are in this together*, fostering a united team front.

Dealing with Resistance to Collaboration

Resistance to collaborative work environments can arise from various sources, including past experiences, fear of overshadowing, or a lack of trust. Addressing this resistance involves:

- Demonstrating the benefits of collaboration through positive outcomes.
- Encouraging open communication about concerns and hesitations. Brainstorming is a good technique to get ideas flowing. No judgement- just a listing of what comes up for the group.

- Providing opportunities for resistant individuals to experience successful collaboration in low-stakes settings.

Addressing Conflicts through Role Play

Role play, a technique borrowed from improv, can be an effective tool for addressing conflicts and disagreements within a team. By simulating challenging situations in a controlled environment, team members can explore different strategies for conflict resolution, learn to understand different perspectives, and practice making their partners look good, even in difficult circumstances.

From the Workshop to the Boardroom

Try This:

Mirroring exercise where you will work with a partner. Everybody finds a partner and you're going to mirror what you see your partner doing. This builds communication and drives home the improv principle of your partner being the most important person to you. You face your partner and move as they move. Mainly concentrate on your upper torso. As the partners continue to work together and mirror each other, it should be unclear who is leading and who is following. They start to work as one.

Take Away

Making your partner look good is more than a strategy; it's a culture. When embraced, it transforms the way teams operate, leading to enhanced collaboration, increased trust, and a more positive work environment. By prioritizing support, acknowledgment, and constructive feedback, teams can achieve greater success and satisfaction in their collective endeavors. Jaime Rich and Randy Wight's insights into this principle remind us that the strength of a team lies not just in the talents of individual members, but in how those members uplift and support each other.

"You depend on your partner and they may depend on you to provide them with information about their character. It is a symbiotic relationship."

Jaime Rich/Randy Wight

From the Workshop to the Boardroom

Do you think you know the 10 best communication questions that you should ask for yourself or for your organization?

Jaime and Randy have created a list using their improv lens. Click here to see Randy and Jaime discuss the top 10 questions you should be able to answer to improve your personal and professional communication.

bit.ly/10bestquestions

Jaime Rich, Randy Wight

Chapter 6

There Are No Mistakes-

The Benefits of

Embracing Failure

> "There are no mistakes in Improv. We have no script, no scenery, no props. It's all coming from your head so nobody can say it's wrong!"

Randy Wight/Jaime Rich

In the dynamic and often unpredictable world of improv, one foundational mantra stands tall: *There Are No Mistakes.* This principle is not just a pillar of improvisational theater; it's a powerful ethos for corporate teams striving for excellence in collaboration, change, innovation, and communication. Jaime Rich and Randy Wight, seasoned improv producers, directors, and performers, delve into this transformative concept, illustrating how applied improvisation tools can turn the feared enemy failure into an invaluable ally. We've been known to applaud when someone *messes up.*

The Importance of There Are No Mistakes

At its core, the statement *There Are No Mistakes,* champions the idea that every misstep is an opportunity for growth and creativity. In the fast-paced corporate environment, fear of failure can be paralyzing, stifling the innovation and fluid communication necessary for success. By adopting the improv mindset that every outcome is a steppingstone rather than a stumbling block, teams can unlock a new level of creative problem-solving and collaborative synergy.

The Limitations of Fear

Fear of failure narrows vision, restricts experimentation, and ultimately limits innovation. It creates an environment where team members are hesitant to voice ideas, challenge the status quo, or propose novel solutions. However, when teams embrace the improv philosophy, that mistakes are simply part of the process, it liberates them to explore, innovate, and communicate more openly and effectively. Working through and learning from our mistakes is how we grow and get out of our comfort zones.

Embracing Failure in Communication and Problem-Solving

Communication and problem-solving are at the heart of successful team dynamics. Viewing failure as a constructive element, rather than a setback, fosters a culture of trust and openness. When teams learn to celebrate the learning process, including the missteps, they build resilience and adaptability.

Viewing Mistakes as Opportunities

- Feedback, Not Failure: Every mistake offers direct feedback on our actions, providing a unique learning opportunity.
- Innovation Catalyst: Mistakes often lead to unforeseen solutions, pushing boundaries and fostering innovation.
- Empathy and Understanding: Sharing failures can build empathy and understanding within teams, strengthening bonds.

Reframing Failure Positively

- Growth Mindset: Encourage viewing challenges as opportunities to grow rather than insurmountable obstacles.
- Success Stories: Highlight historical examples where significant breakthroughs resulted from initial failures.
- Constructive Feedback: Cultivate an environment where feedback is constructive and focused on future improvements.

Using Failure to Build Rapport and Trust

- Vulnerability: Sharing personal experiences of failure can humanize leaders, making them more relatable and building trust.
- Collective Problem-Solving: Encourage teams to tackle challenges together, viewing each failure as a collective steppingstone to success.

Responding to Unexpected Challenges

- Improvise and Adapt: Use failure as a prompt to think on your feet, adapting to new information and circumstances with flexibility.
- Preparation for Uncertainty: Regular exposure to small failures prepares teams for larger, unforeseen challenges.

Generating Ideas and Solutions

- Brainstorming without Boundaries: Create a safe space for free-flowing ideas, where *bad* ideas can lead to unexpected solutions. With brainstorming comes no judgement.

- The *Yes, And...*Principle: Embrace every contribution, building upon it to explore new possibilities.

Breaking Through Creative Blocks

- Random Stimuli: Use unrelated mistakes or failures as a springboard for new ideas.
- Role Reversal: Approach problems from a completely different perspective, imagining how a failure in one context could be a success in another.

Testing and Refining Ideas

- Prototype and Iterate: Use failures as checkpoints to refine ideas, understanding that each iteration brings improvement.
- Fail Fast, Learn Fast: Encourage rapid proto-typing to identify and learn from failures early in the process.

Try This:

One Word Story. This is another tried-and-true improv exercise, which works on team building, creating something together. We do a lot of storytelling in improv because knowing how to tell a good story can relate to performing a good scene. Everyone should arrange in a circle. We will then tell a story one word at a time, moving around the circle. When someone wants to end a sentence, they will say *period* and then the first word of the next sentence. The story should have characters and make sense. You will send a word to your partner on either side of you and they will then say the next word in the story until the story reaches a conclusion of some sort. You may have an idea in mind, but your partner may surprise you by using a next word that you didn't anticipate.

From the Workshop to the Boardroom

Take Away

In the improv theater, as in life and business, the notion that *There Are No Mistakes* transforms the landscape of interaction, creativity, and growth. By embracing and learning from failure, corporate teams can foster a culture of resilience, innovation, and effective communication. Jaime Rich and Randy Wight's exploration of applied improvisation tools offers a roadmap for turning the feared specter of failure into the most unlikely of allies, paving the way for unprecedented success and fulfillment.

Jaime Rich, Randy Wight

Chapter 7

THE IMPORTANCE OF THE *PSYCHOLOGICAL SAFETY* OF IMPROV

Jaime Rich, Randy Wight

"Improv provides a warm and welcoming environment for all."

Randy Wight/Jaime Rich

In the realm of applied improvisation, psychological safety is not just a benefit—it's a necessity. Jaime Rich and Randy Wight, with their extensive background in improv, have witnessed firsthand the transformative power of a psychologically safe environment. This chapter delves into how these principles, when applied in the business world, can significantly enhance communication, innovation, and productivity.

The Crucial Role of Psychological Safety in Business

Psychological safety, a term popularized by Amy Edmondson of Harvard Business School, refers to a team climate characterized by interpersonal trust and mutual respect in which people are comfortable being themselves. In such an environment, individuals feel safe to take risks, voice their opinions, and admit mistakes without fear of embarrassment or retribution.

This foundation is critical for fostering an innovative, collaborative, and highly productive workplace. This transcends also into improv and the stage. If an actor does not feel safe or supported by the rest of the group or their partner, they are less likely to move out of their comfort zone and feel free to say any line that comes to them.

Why Collaboration in a Safe Environment Matters in Business

Collaboration in a safe environment allows for the free exchange of ideas, ensuring that all voices are heard and valued. This inclusivity leads to diverse perspectives, richer discussions, and more creative solutions to problems. In a business context, where innovation is often the key to staying competitive, creating a culture of psychological safety can be the difference between stagnation and growth.

Seven Benefits of Psychological Safety for Communication, Innovation, and Productivity

1. Enhanced Team Innovation: Psychological safety encourages risk-taking and experimenting with new ideas, essential for innovation.
2. Improved Communication: Team members openly share information, feedback, and concerns, leading to more effective communication. This open communication can enable groups to reach their goals more quickly and efficiently.
3. Increased Employee Engagement: Feeling safe and valued boosts motivation and commitment

to the team's goals. A happier employee is a more productive employee.

4. Faster Problem-Solving: Diverse ideas and perspectives come to the forefront, speeding up the problem-solving process.
5. Reduced Fear of Failure: Teams view mistakes as learning opportunities, fostering a growth mindset.
6. Higher Retention Rates: A supportive environment reduces turnover by increasing job satisfaction. When an employee feels valued and connected in the workplace, it makes sense that they will stick around longer.
7. Greater Adaptability: Psychologically safe teams are more resilient and adaptable to change, a crucial attribute in today's fast-paced business environment.

Enhancing Collaboration and Fostering Trust through Applied Improv

Applied improv techniques create a microcosm of psychological safety, emphasizing support, respect, and shared experiences. These techniques not only break down barriers and build trust, but also simulate real-world challenges in a low-stakes environment, allowing teams to practice and improve their collaborative skills. Trust in your partner is paramount to being able to deliver a good and successful scene.

Shared Ownership and Business Accountability

The ethos of co-creation inherent in improv—where every contribution builds upon the last—mirrors the collaborative process in successful businesses. This shared ownership fosters a sense of accountability, as each member is invested in the outcome and recognizes their role in achieving it. In business, this translates to a more engaged and responsible workforce, where the success of the team is the success of the individual.

Five Improv Techniques for Building Consensus and Finding Win-Win Solutions

1. *Yes, And...*Technique: Encourages acceptance of others' ideas and building upon them, fostering collaboration and innovative solutions.
2. Listening to Understand: Focuses on actively listening to others' ideas before responding, ensuring all voices are heard. Herein lies the difference between merely hearing and listening fully.
3. Role Play and Role Switch: Encourages empathy and understanding by having participants switch roles, leading to more empathetic decision-making.
4. One-Word-at-a-Time Story: Promotes teamwork and consensus-building as the team collectively creates a narrative, one word at a time. There are no right or wrong answers. The goal is just to produce a story that makes sense, has characters and a plot, etc.
5. Shared Storytelling: Involves creating a story as a group, where each member contributes, demonstrating the power of collective creativity

and decision-making. This differs from one word story simply because participants can say a phrase or a line, not just one word.

The Power of Shared Ownership in Creating Business Accountability

The principle of shared ownership in co-creation is pivotal for business accountability. When teams engage in the co-creative process, each member feels a sense of responsibility for the outcome. This shared ownership ensures that all team members are accountable to each other, leading to higher quality work, greater innovation, and a more cohesive team dynamic. It transforms individual success into team success and aligns personal goals with the organization's objectives.

Try This:

Birthday Line Up. This is a silent exercise that promotes team building. It works on good communication. The members will line up by birthday month and day (not year!). This is all done with silent communication. No talking. The group has to figure out how they're going to communicate and how they're going to line up. When the people are finally lined up, the team leader will ask for their birthdays and see how they did.

Take Away

The principles of psychological safety and applied improvisation offer profound benefits for business environments, enhancing communication, innovation, and productivity. By fostering an atmosphere of trust, respect, and shared ownership, businesses can unlock the full potential of their teams, leading to sustainable growth and success. Jaime Rich and Randy Wight's insights into the intersection of improv and business provide a valuable blueprint for organizations seeking to cultivate a dynamic, collaborative, and resilient workforce.

"Smiling and laughter are part of a universal language that transcends cultural boundaries."

Jaime Rich/Randy Wight

From the Workshop to the Boardroom

More Team Building Exercises and Games!

Download this list of additional ways to engage your groups. Skill building, group development, group cohesion, ways to spark and improve communication within your teams or groups.

bit.ly/TeamBuildingExercises

Jaime Rich, Randy Wight

Chapter 8

IMPROV AND THE *META VIEW* OR OUTSIDE VIEW OF SELF

> "It's when you're true to yourself that resonates with other people."
>
> *Keegan-Michael Key*

In the collaborative and often spontaneous world of improv, understanding how we appear to others—be it a partner, customer, or client—from our own point of view is not just beneficial; it's essential. This chapter, informed by Jaime Rich and Randy Wight's extensive experience in improv, explores the concept of the *Meta View* of self. This perspective is crucial for effective communication, relationship building, and real-time co-creation in both the improvisational theater and the corporate environment.

The Importance of the Meta View in Communication and Co-creation

Meta View, or the ability to see oneself from an external perspective, is a critical skill in improv that directly translates to the business world. It allows individuals to anticipate how their actions, words, and behaviors are perceived by others, enabling more empathetic and effective interactions. This awareness is particularly crucial in customer or client-facing roles, where understanding and meeting the needs of others are paramount. It takes stepping out of yourself and observing yourself the way others may view you.

Four Ways Improv Can Improve Your Perspective

1. Enhanced Active Listening: Improv exercises train participants to listen actively, not just for cues to respond, but to understand and empathize with their partners.
2. Empathy Through Role Play: Taking on different roles helps participants understand diverse perspectives, fostering deeper empathy.
3. Feedback Reception: Improv provides immediate feedback through audience reactions, teaching the importance of adjusting one's approach based on external input. One must be able to adapt on the fly to external stimuli from their partner or the audience.
4. Self-awareness Enhancement: Regular participation in improv exercises increases self-awareness, helping individuals understand how they are perceived by others. Even if there is no audience, there is the rest of the class who are observing and seeing.

The Impact of Perspective on Communication and Relationships

An example of the impact perspective can have is found in a common improv exercise: two performers engage in a scene where each has a secret objective unknown to the other. The audience can see how each performer's actions, intended to achieve their objective, are interpreted in various ways by their partner. This exercise mirrors real-life situations where intentions and perceptions can misalign, highlighting the importance of understanding one's Meta View for effective communication and strong relationships.

Using the Meta View to Improve Communication and Build Stronger Relationships

Meta View allows individuals to preemptively identify and address potential misunderstandings in communication, ensuring that their message is received as intended. This foresight can transform interactions, making them more positive and productive.

By reflecting on how one's words and actions are perceived, individuals can adjust their approach to communicate more clearly and empathetically, strengthening relationships in the process. If we don't step out of ourselves and pause to see the reactions from those around us, we will continue to follow the same patterns of communication which may not always be effective.

Self-reflection and Introspection Fueled by Applied Improv

Applied improv encourages continuous self-reflection and introspection, vital for personal and professional development. This practice can lead to:

1. Increased Emotional Intelligence: Recognizing and understanding one's emotions and how they affect others.
2. Greater Cognitive Flexibility: The ability to see situations from multiple perspectives.
3. Enhanced Creativity: Finding innovative solutions to problems by understanding diverse viewpoints.
4. Improved Conflict Resolution Skills: Navigating disagreements with empathy and understanding.

Challenging Biases and Assumptions Through Improv

1. Exposure to Diverse Perspectives: Regularly stepping into different roles broadens understanding and challenges preconceived notions.
2. Questioning the Status Quo: Improv encourages questioning why things are done a certain way, opening the door to new ideas and approaches.
3. Encouraging Curiosity: Improv exercises foster a mindset of exploration and inquiry, essential for challenging biases.
4. Developing a Feedback Culture: Constructive feedback in improv settings helps individuals recognize and address their unconscious biases.

Embracing Change and Maintaining a Growth Mindset

Understanding and leveraging your Meta View requires a commitment to growth and adaptability. Maintaining a growth mindset, where challenges are viewed as opportunities to learn and change is embraced, is fundamental.

This mindset enables individuals to continuously refine their Meta View, leading to better self-understanding and more effective interactions.

Tying Together Business Relationships with the Understanding of *Meta View*

In business, as in improv, the strength of relationships often hinges on mutual understanding and respect. By applying Meta View, individuals can navigate the complexities of business relationships with greater empathy and effectiveness. This approach ensures that communications are clear, needs are understood, and collaborations are fruitful.

Try This:

Big Booty This is a call and response game. Players form a circle and designate someone as Big Booty. Big Booty leads the game. Starting at Big Booty's right, everyone is assigned to a number, counting up from 1. Big Booty begins the game by clapping a basic 4/4 rhythm and with a simple chant.

All: Big Booty, Big Booty, Big Booty - ooooh yeah

Big Booty: Big Booty! Number 1!

The player with the called number will respond by calling their own number out and then another number, or Big Booty.

Number 1: Number 1! Big Booty!

Big Booty: Big Booty! Number 6!

Number 6: Number 6! Number 7!

Number 7: Number 7! Number 7! (Error!)

All: Ooh snap!!

Rhythm is very important in this game; it doesn't matter what number you call out (except your own number), as long as you keep it within the basic 4/4 rhythm.

Take Away

The principles of improv offer invaluable lessons for the corporate world, particularly in the realm of communication and relationship building. By adopting the Meta View, individuals can enhance their interactions, foster stronger connections, and create a more collaborative and innovative business environment. Jaime Rich and Randy Wight's insights into the intersection of improv and business underscore the transformative power of understanding oneself from an outside perspective, marking a path for personal and professional growth.

"Since there is no set, no props, and no costumes, it is up to you to paint the environment for the audience by seeing and saying."

Jaime Rich/Randy Wight

Jaime Rich, Randy Wight

Chapter 9

Channeling Childlike Essence

> *"Improv gives adults a license to play."*
>
> — *Randy Wight/Jaime Rich*

From the Workshop to the Boardroom

Introduction to *Never Grow Up*

In the world of corporate teams and professional development, the mantra *"Never Grow Up"* may seem out of place. Yet, Jaime Rich and Randy Wight, through their experiences in improvisation, have unveiled the transformative power of embracing childlike qualities for fostering better communication, collaboration, innovation, and navigating change. This chapter delves into how applied improvisation can be the key to unlocking these qualities, leading to a more fulfilling professional and personal life. Being given the gift of play is priceless. We often think if we let ourselves go, let loose, that we make ourselves vulnerable. Will people think we are being silly? Not take us seriously? How fun would life be if we could all be a little playful?

Ten Childlike Qualities for Better Communication

1. Curiosity—An eagerness to learn and understand, asking questions without fear of looking foolish. This goes hand in hand with the edict in improv-*There are no mistakes*. When we relinquish the fear of judgement or retribution if we don't act the right way or say the right things,

we are freer to say what is on our mind, to ask the questions that we want and need the answers to.

2. Wonder—The capacity to be amazed by the mundane, seeing the extraordinary in the ordinary. One phrase that is sometimes said in improv is *Dare to be boring*. Sometimes the best scenes are comprised of two people talking and relating. Nothing extraordinary happens. Inexperienced improvisers have problems with this concept, often interjecting a conflict or cataclysmic event of some sort. The audience can be enrapt with just a simple scene of two people relating on stage.

3. Playfulness—Approaching tasks and challenges with a sense of fun and creativity. Improv is all about fun. Many a student has said that it is the most fun that they have in a day or a week. It is a chance to *play well with others*. Many of Jaime's students have bonded and become friends through this team/group playing journey. She has groups of students who have stayed together and followed her from class to

class because they so enjoy the chance to play with each other. It is a chance to be silly.

4. Adaptability—Being open to change and easily adjusting to new situations, much like a child exploring unfamiliar playgrounds. In improv, you need to allow yourself to be changed by your partner, by the scene and by the surroundings. One often needs to change on a dime if a new idea is thrown at them. Rigidity has no place in improv. This ability to adapt and be flexible does take practice. It is easier said than done for some, but practicing improv paves the road to this happening more easily.

5. Fearlessness—Willingness to take risks and try new things without the dread of failure. This again goes to the adage of *"There are no mistakes"* in improv. One needs to break through their comfort zone and embrace the notion that their ideas will be received without judgement and with warmth and acceptance.

6. Imagination—Utilizing creative thinking to solve problems and brainstorming innovative solutions. This is at the essence of improv. There are no sets, no props, no lines. It is all in our head.

With time and practice comes more creativity and a free flow of ideas. We learn to trust ourselves and our intuition.

7. Empathy—The ability to connect with and understand others' emotions, fostering stronger team bonds. In improv, your partner is the most important person to you. You rely on them, and they rely on you. It is a symbiotic relationship. One actor feeds the other and vice versa. You rely on your partner to *get you* and know what you need.

8. Presence—Being fully in the moment, attentive and engaged, without distractions. One must be in the moment and free of the thoughts in their head to be part of a successful improv scene. When one partner is distracted, it can lead to the downfall of a scene. A partner misses cues and lines sent by the other partner. The scene will end up falling short.

9. Joyfulness—Finding delight in the process itself, not just the outcomes. Having an outlet to laugh is often all that people are seeking when they first come into an improv class, and this is fine! Improvisers don't have to have a goal of being on

stage and/or performing in a troupe, they often just want to laugh and play. Improv interjects this into a person's life. Their day-to-day life may be devoid of other opportunities to laugh and play. Laughter can open the floodgates to other emotions. It can be a jumping off point to the freedom to feel and engage with others.

10. Openness—A readiness to accept diverse ideas and perspectives without premature judgment. As an improv partner, you need to be ready to receive whatever your partner throws at you. You need to receive it, embrace it, add to it and send something back. If you are not open or willing to receive whatever ideas come your way, your partner may end up not feeling supported. The ideas will fall into a vacuum between the two partners-never to reach fruition.

Retaining Childhood Attributes: A Road to Greater Fulfillment

Retaining childhood attributes into adulthood can transform how we live and work. Adults often lose their innate curiosity, wonder, and the ability to play under the weight of responsibilities and societal expectations. However, rediscovering these traits can lead to greater fulfillment. Curiosity drives innovation, wonder fuels resilience. By finding joy in small victories, an open heart cultivates empathy, enhancing team dynamics. Applied improvisation acts as a bridge, allowing adults to tap into these childlike qualities, fostering an environment where innovation and creativity thrive. As stated above, Jaime witnesses this environment being built in all of her classes. The class grows and comes together over time.

Overcoming Adult Barriers with Improvisational Tools

Adult life is fraught with barriers that can stifle creativity and hinder effective communication: fear of judgment, resistance to change, and the loss of spontaneity. Applied improvisation offers a set of tools to dismantle these barriers. By embracing the principles of improv, individuals learn to welcome uncertainty, embrace mistakes as opportunities for growth, and value the process over the product. This mindset shift is crucial for overcoming the rigid structures and fears that limit adult potential.

Improv as Adult Play

Improv is, at its core, a form of structured play. It provides a safe space for adults to explore, experiment, and express themselves without the fear of failure. This playfulness encourages a deeper connection with others, fosters creativity, and promotes mental flexibility. In the context of corporate teams, improv as play breaks down formal hierarchies, encourages genuine interactions, and nurtures a culture of support and innovation. It levels the playing field, and all teammates are equal.

The Role of Playfulness, Curiosity, and Adaptability

Playfulness, curiosity, and adaptability are not just beneficial; they are essential for growth and development. These qualities encourage a mindset that is open to learning, flexible in the face of change, and creative in problem-solving. Applied improvisation exercises these traits, making them stronger and more accessible in professional settings. By channeling these childlike essences, individuals and teams can navigate the complexities of the modern workplace with greater ease and success. Think of the wide-eyed look of a child when they first experience or see...really anything! The world around them is amazing to them and filled with wonders.

A Great Example of Rekindling Childlike Wonder

Consider a corporate team facing a seemingly insurmountable project. Instead of approaching it with dread, they apply *Yes, and*...by accepting every idea without criticism, building upon them creatively. This method transforms the project into a playful challenge, encouraging imagination and enthusiasm. The team not only finds innovative solutions but also enjoys the process, rekindling a sense of wonder and fulfillment often lost in adulthood.

From the Workshop to the Boardroom

Try This:

String of pearls. This is another story telling exercise. We start by asking the *audience* for the title of a story that has never been told. The group members stand in a line. The first person to go comes up with the last line of the story and stands all the way to one side of the room. The next person to go comes up with the first line of the story and stands on the opposite side of the room. Everyone else then fills in all the other lines-close to the end, close to the beginning, in the middle-wherever they think the line fits. Every time someone enters with a line, everyone else repeats their lines, starting with the first line, so the story is being created and recreated. This continues until the last person enters with their line. (This works best with a group of 8 or fewer).

Take Away

Embracing childlike qualities through applied improvisation offers a path to richer, more fulfilling professional and personal lives, by fostering curiosity, wonder, openness, and playfulness. Plus, it's fun!

Chapter 10

LAUGHTER!

The Origin of Laughter Really Is the Best Medicine

The saying *Laughter really is the best medicine* finds its roots in ancient wisdom and has been echoed through the ages by philosophers, physicians, and poets alike. It is believed that the proverbial expression can be traced back to the biblical proverb, *A merry heart doeth good like a medicine, Proverbs 17:22.*

Over time, this concept has been supported by numerous scientific studies illustrating laughter's positive effects on physical and mental health, underscoring its timeless relevance. For many, improv is synonymous with gaiety and laughter. Every improv class Jaime teaches ends up with laughter as a component.

Laughter as a Breakthrough Tool

Laughter has an incredible ability to cut through barriers that hold us back. It reduces stress, eases anxiety, and breaks down social barriers, creating an environment where communication flows more freely. By invoking laughter, we can dismantle fears, encourage openness, and foster a sense of unity and trust within groups, making it an invaluable tool in both personal and professional development contexts. Laughter is universal. It doesn't matter where someone is from or what their native language is. It is understood by all. As well as cutting through personal barriers, it can cut through barriers between different cultures.

Relieving Stress with Laughter: Five Examples

1. Watching a Comedy Show: Immersing yourself in humor can quickly shift your perspective and lighten your mood. How many people do you know that can recite their favorite lines from a comedy show?

2. Laughter Yoga: Combining laughter exercises with yogic breathing helps reduce stress and increase oxygen intake. A great way to practice mind/body fitness.

3. Sharing Jokes or Funny Stories: Creates bonds with others, easing social tensions and reducing personal stress. Usually people can find some common ground in the telling of these stories which brings people together. A story from one person can lead to more and more stories within a group.

4. Playful Activities: Engaging in light-hearted activities or games can stimulate laughter and

joy, promoting relaxation. This is where im-prov comes in. A lot of improv exercises are game based, intending to bring laughter to both the audience and at times the actors!

5. Laughing at Oneself: Learning to see the humor in our own mistakes can help mitigate stress and foster resilience. Being able to laugh at ourselves is a start in the improv journey. If we take ourselves too seriously and overly criticize ourselves, it will be hard to let go and experience the joy of improv,

Improv and the Gift of Presence

Improvisation teaches us to be fully present, effectively silencing the internal noise that clutters our minds. This state of presence, facilitated by the spontaneous and unpredictable nature of improv, allows participants to engage fully with the moment, reducing stress and promoting a sense of well-being. Laughter, a frequent companion of improv activities, amplifies these benefits, creating moments of genuine joy and connection.

Good for What Ails You: The Healing Power of Laughter

The concept of laughter being *good for what ails you* is supported by its documented physiological and psychological benefits. Laughter can improve immune function, increase pain tolerance, lower stress hormones, and boost mood. These effects contribute to a holistic sense of health and well-being, making laughter a powerful adjunct to traditional healing modalities.

The Universal Medicine: Laughing at Ourselves and With Others

Experts across various fields recognize the importance of laughter in improving health and strengthening social bonds. Laughing at ourselves encourages humility and resilience, while sharing laughter fosters community and mutual understanding. This dual nature of laughter, as both a personal and shared experience, highlights its unique role in promoting health and happiness. How wonderful to experience a *good laugh!* We often don't realize how long we have gone without experiencing this until we finally have the chance to let go and laugh.

Improv, Laughter, and the Safe Space to Let Go

Improv comedy creates a unique environment where laughter flourishes, offering a safe space for participants to let go of inhibitions, explore new ideas, and embrace spontaneity. This setting, defined by acceptance and encouragement, allows individuals to experience the liberating power of laughter, facilitating personal growth and community building.

Acceptance Without Judgment: Carolyn Hidalgo's Truth

Carolyn Hidalgo's notion of truth as *a place of acceptance without judgment* aligns perfectly with the ethos of improv and the essence of laughter. Improv encourages an environment where all ideas are welcomed and supported, fostering a sense of belonging and acceptance. Laughter amplifies this effect, creating a bond among participants that transcends differences and nurtures genuine connections.

Command of Space and Persona Through Improv

Improv not only facilitates laughter; it empowers individuals to feel in command of their space and persona. Participants learn to trust their instincts, respond adaptively to the unexpected, and project their ideas with confidence. This control fosters a sense of autonomy and effectiveness, enhancing personal and professional interactions.

Laughter as a Catalyst for Emotional Release

Recent studies have shown that laughter can act as a catalyst for releasing a range of emotions. The act of laughing can trigger tears of joy or relief, facilitate the expression of pent-up frustrations, and open the door to deeper emotional healing. By engaging with laughter, individuals can explore a fuller spectrum of their emotional landscape, leading to greater emotional balance and well-being.

Try This:

Ninja Star. This is about sending and receiving messages effectively. The group will arrange themselves in a circle. The person who starts will hold the *Ninja Star* between their thumb and index fingers. (This is improv magic-we will imagine the ninja star.) They will then make eye contact with someone in the circle. The person will then *throw* the ninja star to that person. The person *catches* the ninja star by clapping. That person then makes eye contact with a different person around the circle and throws the star to them. The play continues on this way. If someone is not paying attention to the throw, the ninja star may end up lodged in them somewhere and need to be pulled out. (Again, all improv magic.)

From the Workshop to the Boardroom

Take Away

Laughter, especially when fostered through the practices of improv comedy, serves as a powerful tool for healing, connection, and personal growth. It breaks down barriers, provides relief from stress, and cultivates a sense of presence and acceptance. In the world of improv, where spontaneity reigns, laughter is both the journey and the destination—a reminder that amidst life's complexities, joy, and levity can be found.

"Laughter can open the floodgates to other emotions.."

Jaime Rich/Randy Wight

About the Authors

JAIME RICH

Jaime Rich, a distinguished leader in the world of prevention and well-being, is a San Francisco Bay Area native, originally from New York. With a Master's Degree in Clinical Exercise Physiology, Jaime spent years pioneering in the fitness and wellness industry before making significant strides in underage substance use prevention. Her impactful work in this vital area earned her prestigious accolades, including the Contra Costa County's People Who Make a Difference Award and the Alcohol Hero Award from the California Alcohol Policy Alliance.

A master of public speaking and presentation, Jaime seamlessly transitioned her expertise into the vibrant world of improv—a realm where she has not only flourished but also ignited her deepest passion. As a celebrated teacher, she mesmerizes students across the Bay Area, many of whom loyally travel from class to class under her guidance. Jaime serves as the creative director, co-producer, and a star performer of *ACT II Improv*, enchanting audiences with her dynamic spontaneity.

Beyond the stage, Jaime finds joy and solace in the company of her energetic five-year-old Bernedoodle, whose spirited antics fill her life with laughter and love. Even amidst her busy schedule of teaching, directing, and performing, she maintains a steadfast commitment to personal fitness, which she considers fundamental to her well-being.

Connect with Jaime at Jaime@spontaneousmind.org to discover how improv can transform your approach to communication, collaboration, and creativity—skills essential for success in any field. Join Jaime Rich and explore the transformative power of improvisation, where every moment is an opportunity for growth and discovery.

From the Workshop to the Boardroom

RANDY WIGHT

Randy Wight stands at the forefront of the speaking and training industry as an authoritative professional speaker, seasoned trainer, and award-winning performer, spanning over three decades. Starting his career in stand-up comedy with North Bay Stand-up Comics, Randy clinched a regional finalist spot in Showtime's *Funniest Person in America Contest™*. His diverse skill set spans across being a published author and a savvy sales and marketing expert, with a proven track record of engaging prestigious organizations such as the *National Security Agency, Major League Baseball's Toronto Blue Jays*, and the *British Olympic Team*.

Beyond his successful career in sales and marketing, Randy has deeply influenced the improv community. Over the past decade, he has not only co-founded *Ready or Not Improv*, but also managed *Act II Improv*, thriving as a performer, producer, and creative director. Currently, as the Executive Producer at *Spontaneous Mind Productions*, Randy orchestrates a variety of engaging improv and comedy shows and classes at the *Campbell Theater* in Martinez, California.

Randy holds a Bachelor of Science from Cal State East Bay and brings over two decades of expertise in the food and beverage sector. His strategic acumen in brand building, leadership, and change management has consistently delivered transformative results, fostering team cohesion and spearheading product innovations across international markets.

An ardent advocate of the collaborative essence of improv, Randy thrives in all facets of performance arts—from stand-up comedy to voiceover and corporate training. His extensive training in both long and short-form improv, coupled with his role as an educator offering dynamic online and in-person workshops for a diverse audience, underscores his commitment to the arts.

Randy's production prowess is evident in his leadership at *Spontaneous Mind Productions* and *Ready or Not Improv*,

From the Workshop to the Boardroom

where he has successfully produced workshops and shows at venues like the *Lesher Theater, Alhambra High School PAB, Pittsburg Community Theater*, and the *Martinez Campbell Theater*.

Randy Wight is a dynamic speaker, a transformative performer, and an innovative brand builder dedicated to driving business growth, nurturing high-performing teams, and leading strategic initiatives to new heights.

The Power of Yes And...Communication Companion Workbook.

Download this concise companion workbook for supplemental information, examples, and exercises. This workbook goes hand in hand with the Yes And...Communication book that Jaime and Randy have created. Short summaries are provided on topics such as The Constant Flow of Change, Make Your Partner Look Good, Spontaneity and more!

bit.ly/yesandworkbook

www.ingramcontent.com/pod-product-compliance
Lightning Source LLC
Chambersburg PA
CBHW050306230526
45471CB00005B/2054

THE ART OF ENTREPRENEUHP

How to Build a billion dollars Business Dat Thrives in Any Market place, Defeat your Competitors & Dominate Masterful Strategies, Navigating Challenges & Achieving Success.

RICHARD N. WILLIAMS

All right reserved. No part of this publication may be reproduced, distributed or transmitted in any form or by any means including photocopy, recording or other electronic or mechanical methods, without the prior written permission of the publisher, except in the case of brief quotations embodied in critical reviews and certain other noncommercial uses permitted by copyright law.
Copyright Richard N. Williams

TABLE OF CONTENTS

Overview of Entrepreneurship..3

- Importance of Entrepreneurial Skills 3
- Chapter 1 3
- The Entrepreneurial Mindset 3
- Cultivating a Growth Mindset 3
- Embracing Risk and Uncertainty 3
- Chapter 2 Identifying Opportunities 3
- Market Research and Analysis 3
- Recognizing Trends and Innovations 3
- Chapter 3 3
- Building a Solid Business Plan 3
- Components of a Comprehensive Business Plan 3
- Setting Realistic Goals and Milestones 3
- Chapter 4 Overcoming Challenges 3
- Handling Failure and Learning from Mistakes 3
- Resilience in the Face of Adversity 3
- Chapter 5 Navigating the Legal Landscape 3
- Understanding Business Regulations 3
- Intellectual Property and Legal Protections 3
- Chapter 6 3
- Financial Management 3
- Budgeting and Financial Planning 3
- Funding Options and Capital Structure 3
- Chapter 7 3
- Marketing and Branding 3
- Crafting an Effective Marketing Strategy 3
- Building a Strong Brand Identity 3
- Chapter 8 Leadership and Team Building 3
- Effective Leadership Qualities 3
- Fostering a Positive and Productive Team Culture 3
- Chapter 9 3
- Scaling the Business 3
- Strategies for Growth and Expansion 3
- Managing Scale-Related Challenges 3
- Chapter 10 3
- Case Studies of Successful Entrepreneurs 3
- Examining Real-world Examples 3
- Extracting Lessons and Insights 3
- CONCLUSION 3
- Key Principles and Encouragement for Aspiring Entrepreneurs 3

INTRODUCTION 1

INTRODUCTION

In the clamoring roads of a flourishing city, Abigail, a determined business person, set out on her excursion into the unpredictable universe of business. Her story was not a fairy tale; rather, it was a demonstration of perseverance, creativity, and the art of entrepreneurship.

Abigail's vision emerged when she saw a hole on the lookout - a need ready to be satisfied. Outfitted with her resolute soul and a notepad overflowing with thoughts, she established a tech startup expecting to reform the manner in which individuals associated and imparted.

The first few days weren't all that glamorous. Restless evenings and limited financial plans turned into Abigail's steady friends. The difficulties were overwhelming, from tying down financing to gathering a skillful group. Notwithstanding, it was these moves that filled her assurance to advance and change her fantasies into the real world.

The main advancement came when Abigail effectively tested out her plan to a gathering of financial backers. Their help gave the genuinely necessary monetary lift, permitting her to transform her vision into an unmistakable item. The excursion, nonetheless, was a long way from going great.

As the startup picked up speed, unexpected difficulties arose. A mechanical error took steps to crash the whole undertaking. Rather than capitulating to surrender, Abigail considered it to be an open door to feature the strong soul that characterized her pioneering venture. She mobilized her group, encouraging a climate where inventive critical thinking turned into the standard. Together, they defeated the snag, arising more grounded and more joined together.

Exploring the serious scene requested nonstop development. Abigail urged her group to break new ground, encouraging a culture where each thought, regardless of how unusual, was given thought. This creative methodology put her organization aside as well as drawn in top abilities anxious to add to something notable.

Achievement, nonetheless, was not without its penances. Extended periods of time and steady devotion negatively affected Abigail's own life. However, she found comfort in the information that her work was affecting lives decidedly. The tributes of fulfilled clients filled her energy and filled in as a sign of the more noteworthy reason behind her enterprising undertaking.

In the midst of the ups and downs, Abigail turned into a signal of motivation inside the enterprising local area. She shared her encounters, underlining the significance of strength and versatility. Her story reverberated with hopeful business people confronting comparative difficulties, imparting in them the conviction that achievement was an objective as well as an excursion fashioned through persistence.

The defining moment came when a large company perceived the capability of Abigail's startup and communicated interest in an organization. The discussions were serious, however Abigail stayed undaunted, guaranteeing that the substance of her vision was safeguarded. The cooperation ended up being a unique advantage, catapulting her organization higher than ever of progress.

Abigail's story is a demonstration of the craft of business - an excursion set apart by development, strength, and faithful assurance. Her groundbreaking effect on the business impacted the manner in which individuals associated as well as enlivened another age of business people to set out on their extraordinary excursions, furnished with the conviction that difficulties are not road obstructions but rather open doors for development. In the embroidery of business, Abigail's story stays a clear string, winding through the texture of motivation and win.

Overview of Entrepreneurship

Business is a dynamic and multi-layered idea that assumes an urgent part in driving monetary development, encouraging development, and forming the business scene. At its center, business includes the recognizable proof and quest for amazing chances to make esteem through the creation or change of items, administrations, or cycles. This overview examines the definitions, characteristics, types, difficulties, and effects on society of entrepreneurship.

Definition and Qualities of Business:
Business is much of the time characterized as the most common way of beginning and working another undertaking, facing monetary dangers and challenges to the point of creating a gain. In any case, the extent of business reaches out past simple business possession. Innovation, risk-taking, adaptability, and the capacity to seize opportunities in a dynamic environment are all hallmarks of this mindset and set of skills.

A strong desire for success, a willingness to take calculated risks, a propensity for innovation, and the capacity to learn from mistakes are essential traits of successful entrepreneurs. Passion for their ideas and a desire to see positive change are often the driving forces behind entrepreneurs. They show flexibility despite challenges and have powerful correspondence and administration abilities.

Sorts of Business venture:
Enterprising exercises manifest in different structures, prompting the distinguishing proof of various sorts of business ventures. Small business entrepreneurship, scalable startup entrepreneurship, corporate entrepreneurship, social entrepreneurship, and innovation-driven entrepreneurship are just a few of these broad categories.

Independent venture Business: involves starting and running small businesses like restaurants, shops, and service providers in the local area.

Adaptable Startup Business venture: Centers around making and scaling imaginative endeavors with the potential for fast development, frequently determined by innovation or troublesome plans of action.

Corporate Business venture (Enterprise endeavor): Alludes to enterprising exercises inside existing huge associations, where representatives work on imaginative activities and drives to drive inner development.

Social Business: Intends to resolve social or natural issues by making manageable arrangements, frequently through the foundation of charity or for-benefit endeavors with a social mission.

Advancement Driven Business venture: Focuses on making esteem through mechanical progressions, clever thoughts, and the advancement of weighty items or administrations.

The Pioneering System:

The enterprising system includes a progression of interconnected strides, from thought age to the foundation and development of an endeavor. These means are not really direct and may include cycles and variations. The key stages incorporate open door ID, attainability examination, business arranging, subsidizing and funding, execution, and progressing the board and development.

Opportunity Distinguishing proof: Business people spot potential open doors by recognizing neglected needs, holes on the lookout, or arising patterns. Creativity, market research, and a thorough comprehension of customer preferences are required at this stage.

Achievability Investigation: When an open door is distinguished, business people evaluate its plausibility. This includes assessing market interest, contest, functional prerequisites, and expected chances.

Business Arranging: Business people foster a complete field-tested strategy that frames their vision, mission, target market, incentive, and functional methodology. A very much created strategy is significant for drawing in financial backers and directing the endeavor.

Subsidizing and Funding: Business people secure the vital financing to send off and support their endeavors. Money sources might incorporate individual reserve funds, advances, private backers, financial speculators, crowdfunding, or government awards.

Implementation: With the assets set up, business people execute their marketable strategies, frequently experiencing difficulties and adjusting their methodologies in view of true criticism.

Continuous Administration and Development: Effective business people center around proficient administration, ceaseless advancement, and key development. They adjust to advertise changes, influence open doors, and assemble maintainable endeavors.

Obstacles to Entrepreneurship

While business ventures offer various prizes, it isn't without its difficulties. Business people face hindrances that require strength, versatility, and vital critical thinking. Normal difficulties incorporate monetary imperatives, market contests, administrative obstacles, versatility issues, and the intrinsic gamble of business disappointment. Exploring these difficulties requires a blend of business insight, diligence, and a readiness to gain from misfortunes.

Effect of Business:

Business has expansive ramifications for people, networks, and economies. A portion of the key effects include:

Financial Development: By creating jobs, encouraging innovation, and increasing productivity, entrepreneurial ventures contribute to economic growth. Fruitful new companies can altogether affect Gross domestic product development.

Development and Mechanical Headway: Business visionaries are frequently at the cutting edge of development, presenting new items, administrations, and advancements that disturb existing business sectors and add to generally speaking advancement.

Work Creation: The creation of new jobs is greatly aided by small and medium-sized businesses (SMEs), many of which are run by business owners. They are adequately lithe to adjust to changing economic situations and add to work open doors.

Local area Advancement: Nearby organizations, particularly those started by business people, add to the social and financial texture of networks. They give labor and products, support neighborhood drives, and make a feeling of character.

Worldwide Intensity: A nation's global competitiveness is enhanced by international expansion of entrepreneurial ventures. They contribute to a more interconnected global economy by bringing diverse perspectives, encouraging collaboration, and doing so.

Social Effect: Poverty, inequality, and environmental sustainability are just a few of the pressing social issues addressed by social entrepreneurship. These endeavors expect to make positive change and enduring effect past monetary achievement.

Entrepreneurship is a dynamic force that propels advancements in technology, society, and the economy. Business visionaries, with their imaginative soul and hazard taking mentality, shape the business scene and add to the prosperity of social orders. Overcoming obstacles, seizing opportunities, and having a long-lasting impact on individuals, communities, and the global economy are all part of the entrepreneurial journey. As the enterprising biological system keeps on developing, its importance in molding the eventual fate of business and society stays unquestionable.

Importance of Entrepreneurial Skills

Pioneering abilities assume an urgent part in driving development, financial development, and cultural turn of events. The significance of these abilities stretches out past conventional undertakings, impacting different parts of expert and individual life. In a quickly developing worldwide scene, people furnished with pioneering abilities are better situated to explore difficulties, distinguish potential open doors, and add to positive change.

At the center of enterprising abilities lies the capacity to think fundamentally and inventively. Business people have a special mentality that empowers them to see prospects where others could see impediments. This attitude encourages critical abilities to think, permitting people to move toward difficulties with strength and creativity. In a world set apart by vulnerability and consistent change, the ability to adjust and improve is critical, making enterprising abilities exceptionally pursued.

One vital part of innovative abilities is powerful correspondence. Business visionaries should explain their thoughts plainly to financial backers, clients, and colleagues. This expertise not just works with the fruitful send off of a business yet in addition assumes a fundamental part in building enduring connections. Compelling correspondence upgrades cooperation, diminishes misconceptions, and encourages a positive workplace, which are all fundamental components for manageable progress in any field.

Besides, innovative abilities include serious areas of strength for an of drive and a readiness to proceed with carefully weighed out courses of action. Business visionaries comprehend that progress frequently includes getting out of one's usual range of familiarity. Innovation and the creation of groundbreaking concepts and solutions are fueled by this willingness to take risks. Entrepreneurs are more likely to challenge the status quo and push boundaries, whether they are starting a new business or introducing a novel idea into an existing organization.

Monetary proficiency is one more pivotal part of pioneering abilities. Business visionaries should be adroit at overseeing assets, grasping fiscal summaries, and pursuing informed choices to guarantee the practicality and productivity of their endeavors. This monetary keenness isn't simply relevant to business tries but on the other hand is useful in private monetary administration, adding to in general monetary prosperity.

Pioneering abilities are intently attached to administration characteristics. Effective business people move and propel others, driving groups toward shared objectives. In this context, leadership necessitates not only the capacity to make decisions but also a keen awareness of one's own capabilities and limitations. Entrepreneurs frequently set an example for their teams by demonstrating the values they want to instill. These administration abilities stretch out past business settings, emphatically affecting different parts of the local area and social commitment.

In the present interconnected world, mechanical education is a non-debatable part of enterprising abilities. Business visionaries influence innovation to smooth out processes, contact more extensive crowds, and remain in front of the opposition. Embracing computerized apparatuses and remaining informed about mechanical progressions is fundamental for staying serious in essentially every industry. The foundation of entrepreneurial success is technological proficiency, whether launching an e-commerce platform or using data analytics to make informed decisions.

Coordinated effort and systems administration are indispensable features of innovative abilities. Business visionaries perceive the benefit of building a different organization of contacts, going from guides and counsels to possible partners and clients. Organizing gives admittance to significant experiences, open doors, and emotionally supportive networks that can move a singular's vocation or business forward. The capacity to interface with others, develop connections, and team up on projects is important in this present reality where achievement is much of the time an aggregate exertion.

Moreover, the pioneering soul reaches out past the business domain into social business ventures. People with pioneering abilities frequently try to address cultural difficulties, utilizing their inventive mentality to make a positive social effect. Social business people tackle issues like neediness, training, and natural manageability, adding to the improvement of networks on a worldwide scale.

the significance of pioneering abilities couldn't possibly be more significant in the present dynamic and cutthroat world. These abilities engage people to explore intricacy, drive development, and make positive change. Whether applied in business, innovation, social drives, or self-awareness, pioneering abilities are an impetus for development, flexibility, and achievement. As society keeps on advancing, encouraging and developing these abilities will be fundamental for people and networks to flourish in an always evolving scene.

Chapter 1
The Entrepreneurial Mindset

The enterprising outlook is a strong power that drives people to think imaginatively, face challenges, and immediately jump all over chances chasing development and achievement. Not restricted to those who start their own organizations; rather, it envelops a perspective and moving toward difficulties that can be applied in different parts of life. This outlook is described by a few critical qualities and mentalities that put business people aside from others.

One of the crucial parts of the pioneering mentality is an eagerness to face challenges. Business visionaries comprehend that achievement frequently includes venturing outside one's usual range of familiarity and embracing vulnerability. This chance taking mindset is powered by a blend of certainty, strength, and a faith in one's capacity to beat obstructions. Business people view disappointment not as a misfortune, but rather as an important opportunity for growth that moves them forward. They know that every failure teaches them new things that help them grow as a person.

Notwithstanding risk-taking, business visionaries have a sharp feeling of chance. They are continually watching out for holes on the lookout, issues to settle, or creative thoughts that can prompt business or self-awareness. They are able to take advantage of opportunities that others might overlook due to their opportunistic outlook. Business visionaries are proficient at recognizing patterns, understanding shopper needs, and predicting expected changes in the business scene.

A solid innovative outlook is likewise described by inventiveness and a readiness to shake things up. Entrepreneurs approach challenges from a new angle and are natural problem solvers. They won't hesitate to address existing standards and look for offbeat arrangements. This imagination is fundamental for development, as business visionaries endeavor to make new items, administrations, or plans of action that hang out in a cutthroat climate.

Business people display a serious level of self-inspiration and drive. Not at all like the individuals who sit tight for valuable chances to come their direction, business people effectively search out conceivable outcomes and step up to the plate and transform their thoughts into the real world. This self-propelled approach is powered by a profound energy for their work and a solid feeling of direction. Business people are much of the time directed by a dream that goes past monetary achievement, including a longing to have a beneficial outcome on the world.

Versatility is one more key part of the innovative outlook. The ability to adapt to new technologies, market trends, and consumer preferences is essential for success in today's rapidly shifting business landscape. Business people rush to embrace change and view it as an open door instead of a danger. They are able to stay ahead of the curve and respond quickly to challenges thanks to their adaptability.

Powerful relational abilities are likewise indispensable to the innovative outlook. It is essential for entrepreneurs to be able to articulate their vision, persuade stakeholders, and cultivate enduring connections with partners, investors, and customers. Whether trying out a plan to financial backers or arranging an agreement, viable correspondence is a foundation of enterprising achievement.

Another important part of having an entrepreneurial mindset is networking. Business people perceive the benefit of building major areas of strength for an organization to acquire backing, bits of knowledge, and potential open doors. Organizing gives admittance to tutors, possible teammates, and important assets that can add to both individual and expert development.

Ingenuity is a sign of the innovative mentality. The excursion of a business visionary is frequently laden with difficulties, mishaps, and snapshots of vulnerability. Successful entrepreneurs, on the other hand, are distinguished by their capacity to persevere in the face of adversity. Whether it's exploring a subsidizing dry season, defeating an item to send off misfortune, or confronting a furious contest, business people show versatility and assurance.

The enterprising mentality isn't restricted to business attempts alone; it very well may be applied to different parts of life. People with this outlook approach difficulties with an uplifting perspective, view disappointments as any open doors for development, and stay versatile notwithstanding change. Whether chasing after a profession, individual objectives, or cultural effect, the enterprising outlook gives a significant structure to exploring the intricacies of the present powerful world. The innovative outlook incorporates a bunch of perspectives and characteristics that drive people to think innovatively, face challenges, and quickly jump all over chances. From an eagerness to face challenges and a sharp feeling of chance to imagination, flexibility, successful correspondence, systems administration, tirelessness, and self-inspiration, the pioneering mentality is a strong power that can be applied in different parts of life. By embracing this attitude, people can explore difficulties, seek after advancement, and make progress in their chosen paths.

Cultivating a Growth Mindset

In the fields of psychology, education, and personal growth, the concept of a growth mindset has gained prominence. Authored by clinician Song Dweck, the term alludes to the conviction that one's capacities and knowledge can be created through commitment, difficult work, and learning. Interestingly, a decent mentality expects that these characteristics are inborn and unchangeable. Developing a development outlook can significantly affect individual achievement, strength, and by and large prosperity.

Understanding that challenges and setbacks are opportunities for learning and improvement rather than signs of inherent limitations is the foundation of a growth mindset. Embracing this outlook cultivates an inspirational perspective toward exertion and the educational experience itself. Here are key procedures to develop and support a development outlook in different parts of life.

1. Embrace Difficulties

People with a development outlook consider difficulties to be potential chances to develop and create. Rather than keeping away from troublesome assignments, they tackle them head-on, realizing that the experience will improve their abilities and information. This approach constructs strength as well as extends the limits of what one can accomplish.

2. In a growth mindset, constructive criticism

is viewed as constructive feedback rather than a personal attack. Embracing criticism, whether positive or negative, gives a chance to refine abilities and improve execution. It is absolutely necessary to separate one's personal identity from the critique and concentrate on the possibility of improvement.

3. Exertion is the Way to Authority

In a development mentality, the accentuation is on the cycle as opposed to the result. Exertion is viewed as an urgent element for progress. This outlook urges people to continue notwithstanding difficulties and misfortunes, perceiving that supported exertion prompts authority and accomplishment.

4. Develop Interest

Interest powers a development mentality by encouraging an adoration for learning. Those with a development mentality are normally inquisitive and consider the world to be a valuable chance to investigate and find. Their knowledge is not only enhanced by their curiosity, but it also opens doors to new options and perspectives.

5. Underline the Force of "Yet"

"However" holds huge significance in a development mentality. While confronting a test or misfortune, adding "yet" to the furthest limit of a sentence changes an assertion of limit into a statement of potential. "I haven't mastered this skill yet," for instance, is changed to "I haven't mastered this skill yet," which emphasizes the belief in continued development.

6. Observe Exertion, Not Simply Achievement

In a development outlook, achievement isn't exclusively estimated toward the outcome yet additionally by the work contributed. Recognizing and commending the interaction energizes an uplifting outlook toward difficult work and determination. This approach encourages a feeling of achievement no matter what the result, advancing inspiration and proceeding with exertion.

7. A growth mindset is built on a love of learning that is acquired over time. This mindset actively seeks opportunities to expand their knowledge and skills through self-directed study, formal education, or experiential learning. The confidence in the potential for development keeps them taking part in a long lasting excursion of learning.

8. Encircle Yourself with Development Disapproved of People

The impact of the social climate is significant. Developing a development mentality is built up by communicating with other people who share comparable convictions. A positive feedback loop that strengthens the collective commitment to a growth-oriented mindset is created by participating in discussions, working together on projects, and supporting one another's development.

9. Center around the Method involved with Learning

A development outlook moves the concentration from fixed thoughts regarding insight or ability to the most common way of learning itself. People are encouraged to adopt effective learning strategies, seek challenges, and persevere despite setbacks when they realize that abilities can be acquired over time.

10. Develop Resilience

A growth mindset relies heavily on one's capacity for resilience. People with this outlook view disappointments and misfortunes as transitory and gain from them to adjust and get to the next level. This flexibility improves close to home prosperity as well as empowers people to return more grounded not entirely set in stone to conquer future difficulties.

developing a development mentality is an extraordinary excursion that requires cognizant exertion and responsibility. Embracing difficulties, esteeming exertion, and cultivating an adoration for learning are fundamental parts of this outlook. By embracing these procedures and integrating them into day to day existence, people can open their true capacity for development, strength, and achievement. Keep in mind, the excursion of self-awareness is progressing, and each step taken toward a development mentality brings potential open doors for persistent learning and improvement.

Embracing Risk and Uncertainty

Embracing hazard and vulnerability is a key part of individual and expert development. In a world that is continually developing and introducing new difficulties, the people who valiantly explore the obscure frequently wind up at the very front of advancement and achievement. This eagerness to step into the domain of vulnerability requires an outlook that acknowledges the intrinsic dangers as well as considers them to be open doors for learning and improvement.

Risk is fundamentally a necessary component of progress. Individuals and organizations remain confined to the familiar and secure if they do not take risks. Whether it's chasing after another vocation, beginning a business, or wandering into strange regions, embracing risk is the impetus for change. It fosters resilience and adaptability by opening doors to new possibilities and pushing people to their limits.

The feeling of dread toward the obscure is a typical human sense, frequently pulled in a craving for security and solidness. Nonetheless, the people who oppose this trepidation and decide to embrace vulnerability wind up better prepared to deal with startling difficulties. The capacity to defy and explore uncertainty separates people who flourish in unique conditions from the individuals who stay trapped in the wellbeing of the known.

In the business world, fruitful business visionaries comprehend the significance of chance taking. Silicon Valley, frequently viewed as the focal point of mechanical development, is a demonstration of the force of embracing vulnerability. New businesses rise out of carports with daring thoughts, frequently challenging tried and true ways of thinking. These risk-takers are aware that failing is a necessary part of the process and that each setback presents an opportunity to improve and experiment.

In addition, embracing risk fosters a culture of creativity and experimentation. In a climate where disappointment isn't just acknowledged however embraced, people are bound to consider some fresh possibilities and push the limits of what's conceivable. This attitude cultivates advancement and drives progress, eventually prompting leap forwards that can change ventures.

Vulnerability is an indistinguishable sidekick of hazard, and the two are unpredictably associated. Vulnerability emerges when results are eccentric or obscure, and this very unconventionality makes life and work dynamic and energizing. People should not be afraid of uncertainty; rather, they should see it as a canvas full of possibilities that are waiting to be discovered.

Embracing vulnerability includes fostering a mentality that values flexibility and nonstop learning. It's tied in with being available to change and perceiving that plans might should be changed en route. The people who flourish in dubious conditions are much of the time skilled at rapidly adjusting to new data, utilizing it for their potential benefit as opposed to being deadened by hesitation.

In the individual domain, embracing vulnerability can prompt a really satisfying and significant life. Whether it's choosing to go to an outside country, chasing after a purposeful venture, or making a significant life altering event, venturing into the obscure can achieve self-improvement and self-disclosure. The readiness to embrace vulnerability can prompt a more extravagant embroidery of encounters, widening one's viewpoint and improving versatility.

In any case, it's essential to take note that embracing chance and vulnerability doesn't mean being crazy. Insightful gambling includes an essential strategy, informed direction, and a readiness to gain from the two triumphs and disappointments. It requires a harmony between potentially dangerous courses of action and a sensible evaluation of likely results.

embracing hazard and vulnerability is an outlook that impels people and associations toward development and development. It includes venturing beyond safe places, standing up to the obscure with boldness, and reviewing difficulties as any open doors for learning.

Whether in business or individual undertakings, the people who embrace hazard and vulnerability position themselves to make due as well as flourish in an always impacting world.

Chapter 2
Identifying Opportunities

Distinguishing potential open doors is a vital expertise that rises above different parts of life, from self-improvement to business achievement. Potential open doors resemble unlikely treasures ready to be found, and the individuals who can definitely recognize them frequently end up on the way to accomplishment and satisfaction. In this investigation of distinguishing amazing open doors, we will dig into the outlook, techniques, and useful advances that can improve one's capacity to perceive and profit by openings in assorted situations.

Developing a mindset of curiosity and openness is fundamental to opportunities identification. An inquisitive brain is normally receptive to spotting prospects that others could ignore. It is tied in with being responsive to change, remaining informed, and reliably looking for new viewpoints. This mentality can be sustained through persistent picking up, embracing difficulties, and survey mishaps as learning open doors.

To find opportunities in business, you need to know a lot about market trends, customer needs, and the competition. Statistical surveying turns into a critical device, permitting people and associations to assemble important information that can reveal holes on the lookout or regions where improvement is required. Those who are skilled at seizing opportunities are distinguished by their capacity to interpret this data and identify patterns.

Furthermore, opportunities are discovered in large part through networking. Building significant associations with a different scope of individuals opens ways to an abundance of data and likely joint efforts. Fortunate minutes frequently emerge from systems administration, prompting surprising open doors that probably won't have been obvious through conventional channels.

Imagination is one more fundamental part of perceiving potential open doors. Considering new ideas permits people to imagine conceivable outcomes that may not adjust to regular standards. This attitude shift empowers critical thinking and development, making openings where others could see impediments. Imaginative reasoning includes embracing equivocalness and being alright with vulnerability, attributes that engage people to really explore dynamic conditions.

In order to find opportunities, it is essential to take a proactive approach. Rather than sitting tight for valuable chances to introduce themselves, proactive people effectively search them out. This can include taking on new difficulties, chipping in for projects, or investigating unknown regions. By effectively captivating with their environmental elements, people increment their possibilities coincidentally finding open doors that line up with their objectives.

Timing is in many cases a basic consideration quickly jumping all over chances. Perceiving the right second to act requires a blend of instinct and vital reasoning. It includes evaluating the ongoing scene, expecting future patterns, and understanding when to exploit what is happening. This expertise creates experience and a profound consciousness of the setting in which open doors emerge.

Also, developing versatility is fundamental notwithstanding difficulty. Difficulties and misfortunes are unavoidable, however strong people view them as any open doors for development. People with a resilient mindset can bounce back stronger and be better prepared for future opportunities by adapting to change and learning from mistakes.

Distinguishing open doors isn't restricted to expert or business settings; it reaches out to self-awareness too. Perceiving open doors for personal development, learning, and self-awareness is crucial for driving a satisfying life. This can include searching out new encounters, defining aggressive objectives, and embracing difficulties that push one's limits.

distinguishing open doors is a complex expertise that incorporates mentality, methodology, and activity. Whether in business, self-improvement, or different parts of life, the people who succeed at perceiving potential open doors share normal qualities like interest, flexibility, imagination, and a proactive methodology. By encouraging these characteristics and taking on a mentality that embraces change and vulnerability, people position themselves to uncover stowed open doors and outline a course toward progress and satisfaction.

Market Research and Analysis

Statistical surveying and examination assume crucial parts in the progress of business visionaries. These cycles give significant bits of knowledge into the elements of the market, empowering business visionaries to pursue informed choices and foster systems that line up with shopper needs. In this investigation, we dive into the meaning of statistical surveying and examination for business people, looking at how these devices shape business achievement.

Understanding Statistical surveying:
Statistical surveying is the efficient social occasion, recording, and investigation of information connected with a particular market, industry, or item. For business people, this cycle is much the same as a compass directing them through the mind boggling business scene. It includes concentrating on shopper conduct, recognizing market drifts, and assessing serious scenes. The essential objective is to acquire an exhaustive comprehension of the market climate wherein the business visionary works.

1. Purchaser Bits of knowledge:
Statistical surveying gives business people a profound comprehension of

shopper inclinations, ways of behaving, and needs. Entrepreneurs can tailor their products or services to meet specific customer needs by conducting surveys, interviews, and analyzing purchasing patterns. This client driven approach improves consumer loyalty as well as encourages brand dependability.

2. Identifying Possibilities:

Markets with unmet needs or gaps in existing products or services are frequently targeted by entrepreneurs. Through statistical surveying, business visionaries can recognize these valuable open doors. Whether it's a specialty market or an imaginative answer for a typical issue, research permits business people to situate themselves decisively and benefit from undiscovered regions.

3. Cutthroat Examination:

Understanding contenders is significant for any business visionary. Statistical surveying helps in evaluating the qualities and shortcomings of contenders, recognizing market holes, and forming procedures to acquire an upper hand. This information is essential for situating items or administrations really and creating extraordinary selling recommendations.

The Course of Market Examination:

Market examination is the following stage subsequent to social event information through statistical surveying. Interpreting the data, recognizing patterns, and making inferences that can help businesses make better decisions are all part of this process. This is the way market examination helps business people:

1. SWOT Examination:

A fundamental part of market analysis is a SWOT (Strengths, Weaknesses, Opportunities, Threats) analysis. Entrepreneurs look at their own advantages and disadvantages, as well as the market's opportunities and threats. This essential assessment helps in fostering a guide for the business.

2. Market Division:
Every customer is different. Market examination permits business visionaries to section their ideal interest group in light of socio economics, psychographics, and conduct. By promoting procedures to explicit sections, business visionaries can upgrade their endeavors and assets for greatest effect.

3. Estimating Methodologies:
Deciding the right cost for an item or administration is a fragile equilibrium. Market investigation assists business people with understanding the value versatility of their contributions and how buyers see esteem. This knowledge is significant for setting cutthroat yet beneficial costs.

4. Pattern Examination:
Market investigation includes following patterns that can influence the business. Being aware of trends enables business owners to adapt and stay ahead of the curve in response to technological advancements, shifts in consumer preferences, or changes in regulations.

True Utilizations of Statistical surveying and Examination:
1. New Item Advancement:
New products and services are frequently developed with significant resources by entrepreneurs. Statistical

surveying helps in distinguishing whether there's an interest for the proposed offering, what highlights buyers' worth, and how it looks at existing other options. This reduces the possibility of introducing a product that may not be well received by the market.

2. Extension Systems:
For business visionaries hoping to extend their organizations, whether geologically or by expanding their product offering, statistical surveying is fundamental. Grasping the new market's subtleties, shopper inclinations, and cutthroat scene is urgent for effective extension.

3. Risk Moderation:
Risk is part of being an entrepreneur, but market research and analysis offer a safety net. By expecting market shifts, monetary slumps, or changes in buyer conduct, business people can proactively change their systems to successfully explore difficulties.

4. Advertising Adequacy:
A first rate showcasing effort can essentially influence a business' prosperity. Market examination assists business people with assessing the viability of their showcasing endeavors. By estimating key execution pointers and shopper reaction, business visionaries can refine their promoting methodologies for ideal outcomes.

Considerations and Challenges:
Despite their effectiveness, market research and analysis present obstacles for business owners.

1. Constraints on Cost and Resources:
Little new companies might battle with restricted spending plans and assets,

making extensive statistical surveying appear to be overwhelming. Nonetheless, even with limitations, business visionaries can use practical strategies like web-based studies, online entertainment investigation, and contender insight instruments.

2. Quickly Evolving Markets:
An enterprise experiences quick changes because of mechanical progressions or moving customer inclinations. To remain relevant in dynamic environments, entrepreneurs need to remain adaptable and frequently update their market analyses.

3. Adjusting Information and Instinct:
While information driven navigation is vital, fruitful business people frequently join information with instinct. Finding some kind of harmony is a continuous test, as depending entirely on information might ignore creative open doors.

In the pioneering venture, statistical surveying and examination act as directing lights. They provide entrepreneurs with the knowledge they need to make educated choices, reduce risks, and take advantage of opportunities. Whether sending off another endeavor, extending a current one, or adjusting to showcase changes, the bits of knowledge acquired through these cycles are significant. Entrepreneurs are better positioned for long-term success in an ever-changing business environment if they embrace the continuous cycle of market research and analysis.

Recognizing Trends and Innovations

Perceiving patterns and developments in business is fundamental for remaining ahead in the always advancing business scene. Business visionaries who have the capacity to distinguish and use arising patterns are better situated to make fruitful endeavors. In this investigation, we'll dive into the critical parts of perceiving patterns and developments in business ventures and how this mindfulness adds to business achievement.

Grasping the Significance of Patterns:

Business visionaries work in unique conditions where purchaser inclinations, innovation, and economic situations are in consistent transition. Perceiving patterns permits business visionaries to expect changes in these variables, assisting them with adjusting their procedures likewise. Whether it's mechanical progressions, changes in buyer conduct, or developing business sectors, remaining receptive to patterns gives an upper hand.

Analyses of data and market research:

Powerful pattern acknowledgment starts with careful statistical surveying and information examination. Business people should assemble important data about their industry, main interest group, and contenders. This includes concentrating on market reports, customer reviews, and breaking down authentic information. By understanding the ongoing scene, business people can recognize examples and expect open doors.

Mechanical Progressions:

Innovation assumes a vital part in molding pioneering scenes. Business visionaries should be watchful in observing mechanical headways that could affect their industry. This remembers forward leaps for man-made brainpower, blockchain, mechanical technology, and other groundbreaking advances. Incorporating these advancements into plans of action can prompt expanded effectiveness and intensity.

Preferences and Behaviour of Customers:

For business owners trying to keep up with changing demands, it's critical to keep an eye on consumer behavior trends. Changes in way of life, values, and inclinations can essentially affect item and administration contributions. Business people ought to intently notice social and social movements, as well as segment changes, to fit their contributions to address the issues of the market.

Emerging Markets and Internationalization:

Business visionaries are not bound to neighborhood showcases, and perceiving patterns on a worldwide scale is progressively significant. Developing business sectors present new open doors, and business visionaries ought to be receptive to financial, political, and social improvements around the world. Entrepreneurs can expand their reach and diversify their customer base by understanding global trends.

Dexterity and Versatility:
Agility and adaptability are exemplified by successful entrepreneurs. Perceiving patterns is just the initial step; business people should turn their techniques in light of the bits of knowledge acquired. The capacity to adjust rapidly to changing conditions is a sign of effective business, guaranteeing that organizations stay important and strong.

Systems administration and Cooperation:
Through networking and collaboration, entrepreneurs can improve their trend recognition abilities. Drawing in with industry peers, going to gatherings, and partaking in cooperative activities give important experiences. Entrepreneurs can collectively identify and capitalize on emerging trends by sharing their experiences and knowledge.

Putting resources into Nonstop Learning:
The business scene is a powerful environment, and business visionaries should put resources into constantly figuring out how to remain informed. This includes remaining refreshed on industry distributions, taking part in studios, and searching out instructive open doors. Trend recognition is closely linked to an entrepreneur's commitment to ongoing education.

Ecological and Social Obligation:
Patterns in natural and social obligation are acquiring unmistakable quality. Business people who perceive the rising significance of supportable practices

and social effect drives can situate their organizations as mindful and ground breaking. This lines up with advancing customer values as well as adds to long haul business manageability.

Contextual analyses and Examples of overcoming adversity:

Examining contextual analyses and examples of overcoming adversity can offer important bits of knowledge into perceiving patterns and developments. Entrepreneurs can gain insight into how certain businesses identified and capitalized on emerging trends by studying the experiences of others. These genuine models give functional illustrations that business people can apply to their own endeavors.

Identifying entrepreneurship trends and innovations is a multifaceted process that necessitates market awareness, technological expertise, and adaptability. The complexities of the business landscape can be navigated and sustained success can be achieved by entrepreneurs who place a high value on staying informed, embracing change, and capitalize on opportunities presented by emerging trends.

Chapter 3
Building a Solid Business Plan

Entrepreneurs use a business plan to map out their vision, mission, and strategies for their business. A solid business plan is essential to success because it provides a structured strategy for achieving objectives and attracting investors. This extensive record regularly incorporates key components that add to its viability.

1. Leader Rundown: The chief synopsis is a compact outline of the whole field-tested strategy, catching the quintessence of your business, its goals, and the market it serves. Even though it appears at the beginning, it is typically written last to summarize the most important points.

2. Business Depiction: This part digs into the subtleties of your business, covering its inclination, reason, and objectives. It contains information about your products or services, target audience, and distinctive selling propositions that distinguish your company from competitors.

3. Market Investigation: It is essential to Grasp the market. Analyze your industry, your rivals, and your target market in depth. Distinguish market patterns, amazing open doors, and expected difficulties. A SWOT analysis of your company's strengths, weaknesses, opportunities, and threats ought to be included in this section as well.

4. Association and The executives: Give an authoritative design enumerating key colleagues, their jobs, and obligations. The management team's expertise and experience should be highlighted in this section, along with how their skills contribute to the company's success.

5. Items or Administrations: Portray your contributions exhaustively. What issue do they settle for your interest group? What makes them remarkable? Include details about the production, delivery, and development phases.

6. Advertising and Deals Technique: Frame your arrangements for advancing and selling your items or administrations. Develop a marketing strategy that includes advertising, promotions, and sales channels and define your target audience. Incorporate a business figure to provide financial backers with a thought of your income projections.

7. Financing Solicitation: Assuming you're looking for financing, obviously express the sum you want and how you intend to utilize it. Detail your monetary necessities, whether it's for startup expenses, development, or working capital. Give a breakdown of how the assets will be dispensed.

8. Monetary Projections: This segment includes making definite monetary estimates, including pay explanations, asset reports, and income articulations.

Utilize verifiable information if accessible and make reasonable suppositions about future execution. Financial backers need to see a way to productivity and profit from speculation.

9. Risk Investigation: Recognize possible dangers and difficulties that your business might confront. Show your familiarity with these variables and diagram systems for alleviating or beating them. This shows financial backers that you've considered the vulnerabilities related to your endeavor.

10. Appendices: Incorporate any extra data or documentation that upholds your field-tested strategy. This might incorporate resumes of key colleagues, statistical surveying information, authoritative records, or some other pertinent material. A well-written business plan is a living document that grows with your company.

Consistently update it to reflect changes on the lookout, industry patterns, and inside improvements.

A very much created marketable strategy draws in financial backers as well as fills in as an important device for directing your business toward progress.

Components of a Comprehensive Business Plan

A thorough marketable strategy fills in as a guide for business people, directing them through the different phases of their endeavor. A very much organized plan helps with getting support as well as gives an essential system to business tasks. To dive into the parts of such an arrangement, it's fundamental to comprehend that it normally involves a few key segments, each tending to a pivotal part of the business. Here are the major parts:

Leader Rundown: At the bleeding edge of the strategy, the leader rundown briefly frames the business idea, mission, and key objectives. It fills in as a depiction for likely financial backers or accomplices, offering a fast outline of the endeavor's reasonability and potential.

Business Portrayal: The business's structure, legal status, and location are all examined in depth in this section. It features the items or administrations offered, the objective market, and the novel incentive that separates the business from contenders.

Market Examination: An intensive examination of the market is essential for understanding the business scene, client requirements, and possible contests. This part frequently incorporates a SWOT examination (Qualities, Shortcomings, Open doors, Dangers) and market drifts that could influence the business.

Management and organization: Financial backers are enthused about the group behind the business. The key personnel, their roles, and qualifications are discussed in this section. A hierarchical graph might be incorporated to outline the design of the organization.

Item or Administration Line: Itemizing the center contributions of the business, this part expounds on the elements and advantages of items or administrations. It might likewise examine any protected innovation, licenses, or remarkable components that add to an upper hand.

Promoting and Deals: Framing the promoting methodology and deals approach, this segment tends to show the field-tested strategies to reach and draw in clients. It remembers data for estimating, conveyance channels, and special exercises.

Financing Solicitation: In the case of looking for outer subsidizing, this part determines the sum required, how the assets will be utilized, and the expected monetary achievements. It furnishes expected financial backers with an unmistakable comprehension of the monetary requirements of the business.

Financial Forecasts: Itemizing monetary figures, this part incorporates projected pay proclamations, accounting reports, and income explanations. It assists partners with figuring out the expected monetary execution and surveys the attainability of the plan of action.

Appendix: Supporting archives, for example, resumes of key colleagues, statistical surveying information, authoritative records, and some other pertinent data are remembered for the supplement. This part permits perusers to dig further into explicit parts of the marketable strategy.

Risk Examination: Recognizing expected difficulties and dangers is pivotal. Strategies for mitigating or managing these risks are outlined in this section, which identifies and evaluates the risks associated with the business.

Plan of Action: The everyday tasks are itemized in this part. It covers regions, for example, creation processes, offices, innovation prerequisites, and providers. Stakeholders gain a practical understanding of the business's operations from an operational plan.

Method of Exit: While it might appear to be untimely, having an obvious leave methodology is fundamental. Whether through an Initial public offering, obtaining, or different means, this part frames how financial backers can hope to acknowledge profits from their venture.

A complete strategy is a powerful report that develops with the business. Every part assumes an essential part in introducing an all encompassing perspective on the dare to likely financial backers, accomplices, and partners. Through a very much created marketable strategy, business people can explain their vision, exhibit vital reasoning, and impart trust in those thinking about contribution to the business.

Setting Realistic Goals and Milestones

Defining sensible objectives and achievements is a key part of individual and expert turn of events, giving a guide to progress and development. In a world that frequently underlines the significance of accomplishing enormous dreams, perceiving the meaning of setting feasible and sensible objectives is critical.

This approach encourages a feeling of achievement as well as guarantees supported inspiration and progress. Regardless, practical objectives are those that line up with a singular's capacities, assets, and imperatives. While desire is exemplary, setting goals that are past one's span can prompt dissatisfaction and demotivation.

Time, abilities, and available resources are just a few of the considerations that go into setting realistic goals. For instance, an understudy seeking to further develop scholarly execution might define a sensible objective of committing a particular number of hours to concentrating on every day as opposed to going for the gold and radical improvement in grades.

Besides, setting practical achievements takes into consideration a continuous and organized way to deal with accomplishing bigger goals. Separating a major objective into more modest, reasonable advances not just causes the general undertaking to appear to be less overwhelming yet additionally gives a make way forward.

This steady movement permits people to construct certainty as they effectively achieve every achievement, supporting their obligation to a definitive objective. Setting attainable goals is crucial to the success of an organization in a professional setting. Organizations frequently utilize procedures like the Brilliant models (Explicit, Quantifiable, Reachable, Pertinent, Time-bound) to guarantee that objectives are both significant and feasible.

Employees are encouraged to set specific goals that are measurable in terms of progress, achievable with the resources available, relevant to the overall mission, and time-bound to create a sense of urgency with this strategy. In the domain of self-awareness, sensible objective setting assumes a significant part in keeping a solid balance between serious and fun activities. Unreasonable assumptions can prompt burnout and stress, influencing mental and actual prosperity. By setting attainable achievements, people can explore difficulties all the more successfully, encouraging flexibility and versatility. It's critical to take note of that sensible objectives ought not be seen as a restriction on one's true capacity. Rather, they act as an essential system for progress. Instead of settling for mediocrity, setting attainable goals encourages a thoughtful and strategic approach to personal and professional development.

An essential part of compelling objective setting is mindfulness. Grasping one's assets, shortcomings, and regions for development is indispensable to creating sensible objectives. Individuals with this self-awareness are able to establish goals that make use of their capabilities and recognize areas in which they may require additional effort or skill development. Likewise, routinely rethinking and it is fundamental to change objectives. Life is ever-changing, and unforeseen events may occur.

Goal-setting that is flexible enables adaptability to shifting circumstances without feeling defeated. This capacity to recalibrate and turn is a critical quality of fruitful people and associations. Besides, outer help and responsibility components can improve the probability of accomplishing reasonable objectives. Offering objectives to companions, family, or partners makes an emotionally supportive network that gives consolation and direction.

Furthermore, looking for mentorship or expert counsel can offer important experiences and point of view, adding to a more complete and sensible objective setting process. laying out practical objectives and achievements is a foundation of individual and expert achievement. It includes a cautious harmony among desire and reasonableness, recognizing individual limitations while cultivating a mentality of nonstop improvement.

Reasonable objectives give guidance, inspiration, and pride, adding to a satisfying and intentional excursion of development and improvement.

Chapter 4
Overcoming Challenges

Defeating difficulties as a business visionary is an inborn piece of the excursion towards building a fruitful business. The pioneering way is filled with hindrances that request flexibility, versatility, and an essential outlook. In this investigation, we'll dig into the different difficulties business people experience and examine viable systems for defeating them.

One of the essential difficulties business people face is the vulnerability of the business scene. Market variances, changing customer inclinations, and unanticipated occasions, for example, financial slumps or worldwide pandemics can essentially influence a business. To explore this vulnerability, fruitful business people focus on remaining informed about industry patterns, leading careful statistical surveying, and staying deft in their business methodologies.

Monetary difficulties are one more typical obstacle for business people. Getting subsidizing, overseeing income, and settling on insightful monetary choices are basic parts of supporting a business. Finding the right balance between investing in growth opportunities and maintaining financial stability is a common challenge for entrepreneurs.

Building a vigorous monetary arrangement, looking for different money sources, and intently checking costs are fundamental stages in beating monetary difficulties. Building areas of strength for an is significant for the outcome of any endeavor, yet it accompanies its own arrangement of difficulties. Business people might confront troubles in recruiting and holding talented experts, cultivating a positive work culture, and successfully dealing with a different group.

Beating these difficulties requires an essential way to deal with enlistment, putting resources into representative turns of events, and encouraging open correspondence inside the association. Advancement is at the core of business, yet putting up groundbreaking thoughts for sale to the public isn't without its hindrances. Business people should explore through the intricacies of item advancement, protected innovation issues, and rivalry. Remaining ahead in the development game requires a pledge to ceaseless picking up, embracing a culture of imagination, and effectively looking for criticism from clients and industry specialists.

Market immersion and serious rivalry present critical difficulties for business people entering laid out enterprises. A distinct value proposition, strong branding, and a thorough comprehension of the requirements of customers are necessary for standing out in a crowded market. Business visionaries should zero in on separation, fabricating areas of strength for a character, and reliably conveying excellent worth to acquire an upper hand. Administrative consistency and lawful issues can likewise make obstacles for business visionaries.

Exploring complex legitimate structures, getting important allowances, and guaranteeing consistency with industry guidelines are urgent for long haul maintainability. Looking for legitimate advice, remaining informed about important regulations, and proactively tending to consistency issues are fundamental stages in beating administrative difficulties. The close to home cost of business ventures ought to be acknowledged with a sober mind. Business visionaries frequently face elevated degrees of stress, vulnerability, and the strain to succeed.

Keeping up with emotional wellness and prosperity is principal for long haul achievement. Creating survival techniques, looking for help from coaches or companions, and encouraging a solid balance between fun and serious activities are indispensable parts of defeating the personal difficulties of business ventures. In today's fast-paced digital environment, adapting to technological advancements is a constant challenge for entrepreneurs.

Embracing new advances, remaining refreshed on industry patterns, and coordinating computerized devices into business tasks are fundamental for remaining cutthroat. Business people should be proactive in taking on innovation that upgrades proficiency, further develops client encounters, and opens new open doors for development. Scaling a business presents its own arrangement of difficulties, including extending tasks, overseeing expanded requests, and keeping up with quality as the organization develops.

Business visionaries should foster versatile plans of action, put resources into framework, and cautiously plan the scaling system to stay away from entanglements. Vital organizations, reevaluating non-center capabilities, and utilizing innovation can work with a smoother scaling venture. The path to becoming an entrepreneur is fraught with difficulties, but overcoming them is essential to success.

Entrepreneurs must accept uncertainty, cultivate resilience, and constantly adjust to the changing business environment. Entrepreneurs can navigate the complexities of entrepreneurship and build thriving businesses by addressing financial, team-related, innovation, market, legal, emotional, and technological issues with strategic foresight.

Handling Failure and Learning from Mistakes

Dealing with disappointment and gaining from botches are essential parts of the innovative excursion. In the dynamic and testing universe of business, difficulties and disappointments are unavoidable.

However, the secret to long-term success is not avoiding failure, but rather effectively managing it and learning from it. One of the principal qualities that effective business people have is strength. They comprehend that disappointment isn't the end yet rather a venturing stone towards development and improvement. Rather than being deterred by difficulties, they view them as any open doors to rethink their procedures, refine their methodology, and eventually become more vigorous as business visionaries.

Embracing disappointment requires a change in outlook. As opposed to seeing disappointment as an individual imperfection, business people need to see it as a characteristic piece of the educational experience. Each difficulty gives an opportunity to dissect what turned out badly, recognize regions for development, and foster a more educated and key methodology pushing ahead.

Experimentation and taking chances are frequently the causes of failure in the entrepreneurial environment. Business visionaries who will proceed with well balanced plans of action are bound to find imaginative arrangements and momentous thoughts. However, it is essential to acknowledge that not all risks will result in success. At the point when an endeavor falls flat, it's fundamental to direct a careful posthumous investigation to figure out the contributing variables and gain from the experience. Gaining from botches includes a mix of lowliness and a development mentality.

Effective business people are available to input and self-reflection, permitting them to adjust and advance. They perceive that flawlessness is impossible and that difficulties are essential for the iterative cycle expected for supportable business development. Disappointment ought not be seen as an impasse yet rather as a redirection. When confronted with affliction, business people ought to evaluate what is going on impartially, distinguish the main drivers of disappointment, and utilize this information to turn or refine their business techniques.

This flexibility is a sign of effective business visionaries who comprehend that the business scene is continually developing, and the capacity to turn is an important expertise. Besides, business people ought to cultivate a culture inside their groups that energizes risk-taking and gaining from disappointments.

At the point when colleagues have a good sense of reassurance to trial and realize that disappointment is acknowledged as a piece of the excursion, it advances development and innovativeness. This positive culture considers the development of groundbreaking thoughts and arrangements, eventually driving the innovative endeavor forward. It's vital to note that not all disappointments are horrendous; some are minor difficulties that offer significant bits of knowledge.

Entrepreneurs should prioritize addressing the most pressing issues and differentiate between various failure levels. By focusing on the aspects that will have the greatest impact on future success, this discernment enables a more targeted and efficient response. Also, systems administration and looking for mentorship can be important in exploring the difficulties of business ventures.

Gaining from the encounters of other people who have confronted comparable obstacles can give important viewpoints and bits of knowledge. Coaches can offer direction on beating snags and offer their own accounts of flexibility, supporting that disappointment is certainly not a sign to offer up yet a chance for development. In the enterprising scene, deftness is a valued quality.

Business people should adjust their techniques in view of market criticism and evolving conditions. Disappointment frequently fills in as an impetus for this flexibility, provoking business people to rethink their plans of action, showcasing systems, or item contributions to line up with market requests. dealing with disappointment and gaining from botches are essential parts of the innovative excursion. Strength, a development outlook, and an eagerness to adjust are fundamental characteristics that effective business visionaries develop.

Embracing disappointment as a characteristic piece of the educational experience permits business people to extricate important illustrations, refine their procedures, and eventually make long haul progress in the dynamic and testing universe of business venture.

Resilience in the Face of Adversity

Business is an excursion loaded with difficulties and vulnerabilities. The capacity to explore through misfortune is a central quality of fruitful business people. Flexibility, in this specific circumstance, isn't just about returning quickly from misfortunes yet flourishing notwithstanding difficulty. It is a quality that distinguishes successful entrepreneurs from unsuccessful ones. In this exposition, we will investigate the meaning of versatility in business venture, how it shapes the enterprising attitude, and the methodologies business visionaries utilize to beat difficulties.

In the first place, strength is an urgent part of the enterprising mentality. The actual idea of beginning and maintaining a business implies consistent gamble and vulnerability. Business visionaries frequently experience hindrances like monetary misfortunes, market unpredictability, and unforeseen rivalry. Resilience serves as a shield in such circumstances, enabling entrepreneurs to weather the storms. It's tied in with keeping up with concentration and assurance when confronted with difficulties, seeing difficulties as any open doors for development as opposed to impossible hindrances.

One key component that adds to versatility in business is a profound feeling of direction. Passion for one's vision and purpose is the driving force behind successful business people. This feeling of direction turns into a strong inspiration during difficult stretches, assisting business visionaries with remaining focused on their objectives. When confronted with difficulty, the business person with a solid feeling of direction is bound to drive forward, tracking down effective fixes and adjusting their procedures to defeat difficulties.

Besides, versatility in business is intently attached to the capacity to gain from disappointment. In the entrepreneurial journey, failures are inevitable, but resolute business people view them as valuable lessons rather than reasons to give up. They dissect what turned out badly, comprehend the elements adding to the disappointment, and utilize this information to work on their methodology. This iterative educational experience is a vital part of strength, as it permits business people to develop and adjust notwithstanding difficulty. One more part of flexibility is the ability to keep a positive outlook. Business people frequently face dismissal, analysis, and incredulity.

Versatile people, be that as it may, move toward these difficulties with an uplifting perspective. They keep an optimistic outlook despite setbacks, which helps them stick with it. Not only does having a positive outlook assist in overcoming difficulties, but it also attracts the support of other people, such as investors, employees, and customers.

Moreover, viable critical thinking is a sign of strong business people. When faced with difficulties, they don't surrender to surrender yet rather center around tracking down viable arrangements. This capacity to think basically, break down circumstances, and devise well thought out courses of action is essential for exploring the intricate scene of business. Entrepreneurs who are resilient approach issues with a problem-solving mindset, encouraging creativity and adaptability.

Vital gambling of the executives is one more element of flexibility in business ventures. Despite the fact that being an entrepreneur necessitates taking risks, successful businesspeople do not simply accept them. They look at potential dangers, make plans for the worst-case scenario, and put strategies into action to prevent bad outcomes. This proactive way to deal with risk the board improves the business person's capacity to climate startling difficulties and guarantees a more steady business establishment.

A key to entrepreneurial success is resilience. The power drives business people forward despite affliction, empowering them to conquer mishaps, gain from disappointments, and adjust to evolving conditions. The foundation of entrepreneurial success is a resilient mindset, a positive outlook, a sense of purpose, effective problem-solving skills, and strategic risk management.

On their way to creating businesses that are both long-lasting and successful, aspirant entrepreneurs ought to be aware of the significance of resilience and cultivate it as a fundamental quality.

Chapter 5 Navigating the Legal Landscape

Exploring the lawful scene is a fundamental part of business, as it assumes an essential part in molding the achievement and manageability of a business. Business visionaries should be knowledgeable in different lawful angles to safeguard their inclinations, agree with guidelines, and alleviate possible dangers. In this investigation of the legitimate scene in business, we will dive into key regions, for example, business structures, contracts, protected innovation, work regulation, and administrative consistency.

Business Organizations: Picking the right business structure is one of the underlying and basic lawful choices for business people. Various designs, for example, sole ownership, organization, restricted responsibility organization (LLC), and company, offer particular benefits and detriments. Although sole proprietorship and partnership offer simplicity, each owner is personally liable. LLCs offer a harmony among effortlessness and risk security, while partnerships give greatest responsibility insurance yet include complex conventions.

Understanding the legitimate ramifications of each design is fundamental for business people to settle on informed choices in view of their business objectives, size, and hazard resistance. Legitimate direction can direct business people through this dynamic cycle, guaranteeing consistency with state regulations and guidelines.

Contracts: Contracts structure the foundation of deals and connections. Business visionaries participate in agreements for different purposes, including associations, seller connections, client arrangements, and work contracts. A very much drafted agreement obviously frames the privileges, commitments, and obligations of each party, forestalling debates and giving a legitimate system to goal in the event that issues emerge.

Business visionaries ought to give cautious consideration to contract subtleties, including agreements, installment terms, debate goal instruments, and end conditions. Legitimate experts can help with drafting and surveying agreements to guarantee lucidity, enforceability, and consistency with pertinent regulations.

Licensed innovation: Safeguarding licensed innovation (IP) is significant for some organizations, particularly those dependent on development, marking, or imaginative works. Business visionaries should grasp the various types of IP, including brand names, copyrights, licenses, and proprietary advantages, and go to suitable lengths to shield their scholarly resources. Brand name enlistment safeguards brand names and logos, while copyrights cover unique innovative works. Licenses award select freedoms to developments, and proprietary advantages include secret business data. Business people ought to proactively recognize and safeguard their IP resources through enlistments, arrangements, and other lawful instruments to forestall encroachment and unapproved use.

Work Regulation: Entrepreneurs need to know how to navigate employment law in order to hire and manage employees. Important aspects include adherence to labor laws, workplace policies, and employment contracts. Business visionaries should know about guidelines overseeing compensation, working hours, separation, provocation, and end methods.

Making a positive and lawfully consistent workplace includes tending to worker privileges, advantages, and obligations. Legitimate guidance can help business people lay out and keep up with HR rehearses that comply with pertinent regulations, decreasing the gamble of work related debates.

Administrative Consistence: Business visionaries work inside a complex administrative climate, dependent upon industry-explicit guidelines, permitting prerequisites, and shopper security regulations.

Remaining consistent with these guidelines is pivotal to stay away from lawful results and encourage a reliable business notoriety. Administrative consistency includes understanding and complying with nearby, state, and government regulations that influence the business. Business visionaries ought to direct normal reviews to guarantee continuous consistency, adjusting to changes in guidelines and proactively resolving expected issues before they heighten.

exploring the legitimate scene in business is a multi-layered challenge that requires continuous consideration and constancy. Business people should be proactive in looking for legitimate direction, whether in organizing their business, drafting contracts, safeguarding protected innovation, overseeing representatives, or guaranteeing administrative consistency. By focusing on lawful contemplations, business visionaries can fabricate serious areas of strength for their organizations, cultivating development and flexibility in the dynamic and cutthroat business climate.

Understanding Business Regulations

Understanding business guidelines is vital for business visionaries and associations to explore the complex lawful scene that oversees their tasks. These laws cover a wide range of rules and guidelines that governments have made to keep the economy stable, protect consumers, and ensure fair competition. In this investigation, we will dive into the meaning of business guidelines, the sorts of guidelines that exist, and the effect they have on organizations.

Significance of Business Guidelines: In order to create a business environment that is both equitable and transparent, regulations are essential. They are intended to forestall deceitful exercises, guarantee moral lead, and keep a level battleground for all members in the commercial center. Without these guidelines, organizations could participate in rehearsals that hurt buyers, exploit workers, or harm the climate. Additionally, regulations provide businesses with a framework within which to operate, providing them with a sense of certainty and predictability. This security is fundamental for long haul arranging, speculation, and manageable development. By complying with guidelines, organizations can fabricate entrust with clients, financial backers, and different partners, which is key for their prosperity.

Kinds of Business Guidelines: Business guidelines can be comprehensively classified into a few sorts, each tending to explicit parts of business tasks. These are some:

Ecological Guidelines: Businesses' negative effects on the environment are the primary focus of these regulations. They set norms for garbage removal, emanations, and asset use to advance supportability and safeguard biological systems.

Work Guidelines: Work regulations administer the connection among managers and representatives, covering angles like working hours, compensation, wellbeing principles, and business contracts. These guidelines mean to guarantee fair and impartial treatment of laborers.

Monetary Guidelines: Monetary guidelines are intended to keep up with the solidness of monetary business sectors. Accounting, auditing, and reporting regulations, as well as banking and securities regulations, are included to ensure fiscal responsibility and prevent fraud.

Regulations for Protecting Consumers: These guidelines shield the privileges of buyers by guaranteeing item wellbeing, fair promoting, and straightforward strategic approaches. They want to stop businesses from being dishonest or unfair, which could hurt customers.

Rivalry Guidelines: Contest regulations are set up to forestall restraining infrastructures and advance fair rivalry. They restrict serious practices, for example, cost fixing, market assignment, and different procedures that block free and open business sectors.

Wellbeing and Security Guidelines: These guidelines are centered around keeping a protected workspace. They set norms for working environment wellbeing, gear, and conventions to forestall mishaps and safeguard representatives' wellbeing.

Licensed innovation Guidelines: Licensed innovation regulations safeguard the freedoms of makers and creators by conceding select privileges to their manifestations. This incorporates licenses, brand names, copyrights, and proprietary advantages, cultivating advancement and inventiveness.

Effect of Business Guidelines: The effect of business guidelines is complex, impacting different parts of an organization's tasks, its relationship with partners, and its general presentation.

Functional Consistency: Organizations should contribute time and assets to comprehend and agree with guidelines pertinent to their industry. This frequently includes carrying out unambiguous strategies, getting licenses, and sticking to detailing necessities. Fines, legal repercussions, and harm to the business's reputation may result from noncompliance.

Trust from Customers: Complying with shopper insurance guidelines fabricates entrust with clients. At the point when organizations are straightforward and responsible in their practices, purchasers are bound to go with informed decisions and stay faithful to the brand.

Advancement and Contest: Contest guidelines support fair market works on, forestalling the development of restraining infrastructures that could smother advancement and breaking point decisions for customers. This encourages businesses to strive for product and service enhancement to gain a competitive edge.

Relations with employees: By ensuring fair wages, reasonable working hours, and safe working conditions, labor regulations foster positive employee relations. Employee contentment rises and the likelihood of labor disputes decreases when these regulations are followed.

Monetary Solidness: Monetary guidelines are fundamental for keeping up with the strength of monetary business sectors. They forestall deceitful exercises, safeguard financial backers, and add to generally speaking monetary dependability by keeping away from monetary emergencies.

Worldwide Business Scene: Organizations working universally should explore an intricate snare of guidelines from various nations. For successful global expansion and avoiding legal issues, it is essential to comprehend and adhere to these regulations.

Understanding business guidelines is fundamental for the maintainability and moral activity of organizations. While consistency might appear to be overwhelming, it is a vital part of dependable business for the executives. By embracing guidelines, organizations can add to a fair and serious commercial center, form entrust with partners, and make an establishment for long haul achievement.

Intellectual Property and Legal Protections

Inventions, literary and artistic works, designs, symbols, names, and images used in commerce are all examples of intellectual property (IP). It is an expansive term enveloping different types of elusive resources that have esteem and are safeguarded by regulation. By granting creators limited rights to their creations, legal protections for intellectual property aim to foster innovation and creativity. This article will dive into the various sorts of protected innovation, the legitimate systems administering them, and the difficulties in implementing these privileges.

Sorts of Licensed innovation

Patents: Licenses safeguard creations and developments, giving creators restrictive freedoms for a particular period. This select right permits innovators to keep others from making, utilizing, or selling their protected creations without authorization.

Copyright: Copyright safeguards unique works of origin, for example, scholarly, creative, and melodic works. It furnishes makers with the restrictive right to imitate, disperse, and show their works. Not at all like licenses, copyright assurance is programmed upon creation, and enlistment isn't needed, despite the fact that it might give extra advantages.

Trademarks: Brand names shield images, names, and mottos that recognize labor and products in the commercial center. They add to memorability and purchaser trust by keeping others from utilizing comparable imprints that could create turmoil.

Proprietary innovations: Formulas, procedures, and other methods that provide a competitive advantage are examples of trade secrets. Dissimilar to different types of IP, proprietary innovations don't need public exposure however depend on the data being kept classified.

Designs: Design rights safeguard the shape, arrangement, and ornamentation of objects' visual appearance. This is especially true in fields like fashion and industrial design where aesthetics are very important.

Lawful Securities Patent Law: In order to obtain exclusive rights, inventors must disclose their invention in detail in exchange for patent protection. International treaties like the Patent Cooperation Treaty (PCT) aim to streamline the application process across multiple nations because the legal framework for patents varies globally.

Intellectual property Regulation: Copyright insurance is programmed upon formation of the work, and the Berne Show guarantees a base degree of security globally. Intellectual property regulations give makers the option to control how their functions are utilized, recreated, and disseminated, and these freedoms commonly keep going for the maker's lifetime in addition to a set number of years.

Brand name Regulation: Brand name enrollment is commonly taken care of by public or provincial brand name workplaces. The enlistment cycle includes showing the peculiarity and non-conventional nature of the imprint. Brand name privileges can endure endlessly assuming that the imprint keeps on being utilized and is appropriately kept up with.

Proprietary innovation Regulation: Proprietary advantage security depends on keeping up with the privacy of the data. Non-disclosure agreements (NDAs) and contractual arrangements are frequently used as legal safeguards to ensure that business partners and employees do not misuse confidential information.

Law of Design: Configuration privileges are many times acquired through enrollment with pertinent licensed innovation workplaces. These freedoms safeguard the visual appearance of a plan for a restricted period, giving makers selective privileges to the tasteful components of their manifestations.

Challenges in Implementation Globalization: With the worldwide idea of business, authorizing licensed innovation freedoms across borders becomes testing. Contrasting legitimate systems and authorization instruments make it challenging to battle encroachment on a worldwide scale.

Digital theft: The ascent of the web has worked with the unapproved proliferation and appropriation of computerized content. Copyright encroachment, particularly as online robbery, presents huge difficulties to customary requirement strategies.

Arising Advances: The fast headway of innovation, including computerized reasoning and 3D printing, presents new difficulties in safeguarding licensed innovation. Deciding possession and authorizing privileges in these settings is an advancing area of regulation.

Counterfeiting: Fake products, going from design things to drugs, represent a huge danger to protected innovation privileges. The underground idea of duplicating tasks makes it moving for specialists to follow and arraign guilty parties.

Lawful Expenses and Openness: Small businesses and individual creators find it difficult to enforce their rights because the legal procedures involved in protecting intellectual property can be costly. This availability issue raises worries about the inclusivity of licensed innovation insurance.

Future Patterns Blockchain Innovation: Blockchain can possibly upset licensed innovation the board by giving straightforward and secure record-keeping. Shrewd agreements on blockchain stages could smooth out the authorizing and move of licensed innovation freedoms.

Man-made consciousness in IP The executives: Man-made consciousness apparatuses are being created to aid the administration and authorization of protected innovation. From recognizing possible encroachments to robotizing routine legitimate errands, simulated intelligence is ready to improve proficiency in the field.

Worldwide Coordinated effort: Perceiving the difficulties presented by cross-line protected innovation issues, there is a rising accentuation on worldwide cooperation. Endeavors to fit licensed innovation regulations and further develop participation among nations expect to make a more strong and successful worldwide structure.

Adjusting Access and Security: Finding some kind of harmony between safeguarding licensed innovation and guaranteeing availability to data and innovation is a continuous test. Discussions go on about the ideal term of security and the effect of excessively prohibitive IP systems on advancement and freedom. licensed innovation and its legitimate securities assume a significant part in encouraging development and imagination. The developing scene of innovation, globalization, and arising legitimate structures requires nonstop variation to address new difficulties.

Intellectual property law and policy will continue to focus on striking a balance between promoting the common good and protecting creators' rights.

Chapter 6
Financial Management

Planning, organizing, directing, and controlling financial activities are all parts of financial management, which is an essential part of any organization. Viable monetary administration is fundamental for the drawn out progress and maintainability of organizations, as it includes going with informed choices to advance the utilization of monetary assets.

One critical part of monetary administration is planning. The anticipated revenues and expenses for a given time period are outlined in a budget, which acts as a road map for financial activities It enables businesses to efficiently allocate resources, set spending priorities, and establish financial objectives. By sticking to a very organized spending plan, organizations can screen their monetary presentation, recognize changes, and make opportune changes in accordance with accomplishing monetary targets.

Risk assessment and mitigation is another important part of financial management. Organizations face different monetary dangers, including market vacillations, loan cost changes, and credit gambles. To safeguard the organization's financial health, financial managers must examine these risks, devise strategies to reduce them, and implement risk management measures. This proactive methodology helps in limiting possible misfortunes and defending the organization's monetary strength. Financial management also relies heavily on investment choices.

Monetary supervisors assess potential venture open doors, taking into account factors like profit from speculation, chance, and economic situations. They plan to allot assets to undertakings or resources that create the best yields while lining up with the association's generally speaking vital goals. Long-term growth and profitability are aided by strategic investment decisions. Capital construction is one more central part of monetary administration. It includes deciding the ideal blend of obligation and value to fund the association's tasks and undertakings.

Monetary directors should figure out some kind of harmony between utilizing obligation for charge benefits and staying away from unreasonable monetary gamble. The right capital structure increases shareholder value, lowes financing costs, and improves the company's capacity to raise capital. A company's day-to-day operations and liquidity are both dependent on effective cash flow management.

Monetary administrators screen cash inflows and surges, foreseeing future money needs and keeping a sufficient money hold. Productive income the executives forestalls liquidity emergencies, empowering the association to meet its monetary commitments and benefit from venture potential open doors.

Monetary detailing and investigation give experiences into an organization's presentation and monetary wellbeing. Exact and opportune fiscal reports, including pay articulations, monetary records, and income proclamations, assist partners with evaluating the association's productivity, dissolvability, and functional proficiency. Monetary examination includes assessing key monetary proportions, looking at execution against industry benchmarks, and distinguishing regions for development. Cost administration is one more fundamental part of monetary administration. It includes controlling and decreasing costs to improve productivity.

Monetary chiefs carry out cost-saving measures, arrange good terms with providers, and improve functional cycles to accomplish proficiency. Compelling expenses the executives adds to higher overall revenues and expanded seriousness on the lookout. Because it involves maximizing the organization's tax position in order to legally minimize liabilities, tax planning is an essential component of financial management. Monetary chiefs investigate charge motivators, credits, and allowances to lessen the general taxation rate. Key assessment arranging guarantees consistency with charge guidelines while boosting after-charge benefits.

Monetary administration isn't restricted to organizations; it is similarly significant for people. Individual monetary administration includes planning, saving, effective money management, and anticipating significant life altering situations like schooling, homeownership, and retirement. People should pursue informed monetary choices to accomplish their monetary objectives and secure their future.

Monetary administration is a complex discipline that includes different cycles and systems to streamline the utilization of monetary assets. From planning and chance administration to venture choices and capital design, powerful monetary administration is significant for the achievement and maintainability of organizations. It includes a consistent pattern of arranging, investigation, and decision-production to explore the complex monetary scene and accomplish long haul monetary goals. A key to financial success and well-being is effective financial management, whether at work or at home.

Budgeting and Financial Planning

Planning your finances and making a budget are two essential steps toward effective and responsible money management. In our current reality where monetary solidity is a critical part of an individual's prosperity, the capacity to plan successfully and plan for what's in store is priceless. This article will dig into the significance of planning, key stages in making a spending plan, and the meaning of monetary anticipating people and families.

How important budgeting is:

1. **Monetary Discipline:** Planning imparts monetary discipline by giving a reasonable system to spending and

saving. It assists people with focusing on their costs and dispense assets carefully, forestalling rash spending that can prompt monetary strain.

2. Obligation The board: A very much created financial plan helps with overseeing and paying off past commitments. Individuals can work toward financial freedom and lessen the burden of high-interest loans by locating areas in which expenses can be reduced or redirected toward debt repayment.

3. Preparation for Emergencies: Planning permits people to save assets for crises. Having a rainy day account guarantees monetary steadiness during surprising occasions, like health related crises or abrupt employment cutback, alleviating the need to depend on layaway or advances.

4. Achievement of Goals: Budgeting lets people set and achieve financial goals, such as saving for a home, education, or retirement. It gives a guide to designating assets towards these goals, guaranteeing progress after some time.

5. Genuine serenity: Knowing where each dollar proceeds to have an arrangement set up gives an inward feeling of harmony. It lessens monetary pressure and tension, permitting people to zero in on different parts of their lives without consistent stress over cash matters.

Key Stages in Making a Financial plan:

1. Pay Appraisal: Start by deciding the absolute pay. This incorporates customary pay sources like compensation, independent income, or different wellsprings of income. Understanding the inflow of cash is essential for viable planning.

2. Cost Following: Record all uses, ordering them into fixed (e.g., lease, utilities) and variable (e.g., food, amusement) costs. Following costs recognizes regions where spending can be changed or diminished.

3. Defining Boundaries: Spending should be prioritized based on needs and objectives. Fundamental costs ought to outweigh everything else, trailed by reserve funds and optional spending. This guarantees that urgent requirements are met prior to distributing assets to unimportant things.

4. Making Classifications: Divide costs into categories like food, entertainment, housing, and transportation. This aids in coordinating the spending plan, making it more straightforward to break down and recognize regions for development.

5. Planning Instruments: Use planning devices and applications to smooth out the cycle. Numerous applications offer elements like cost following, objective setting, and perceptions, making it simpler for people to actually deal with their funds.

6. Customary Survey: A spending plan is certainly not a static record; it ought to be surveyed routinely and changed on a case by case basis. Life conditions, pay changes, and startling costs might expect alterations to guarantee the financial plan stays reasonable and compelling.

Meaning of Monetary Preparation:

1. Long haul Security: Beyond daily budgeting, financial planning focuses on long-term security. This includes putting something aside for retirement, contributing shrewdly, and making a strong monetary establishment that can endure financial variances.

2. Speculation Methodologies: Making investment plans that are tailored to each person's goals and risk tolerance is part of financial planning. This could include expanding speculations across various resource classes to upgrade returns while overseeing risk.

3. Charge Proficiency: A thoroughly examined monetary arrangement thinks about charge suggestions. Individuals can lessen their tax burden and potentially increase their after-tax returns by optimizing tax strategies.

4. Insurance Protection: Monetary arranging includes evaluating and getting proper protection inclusion. This guarantees security against unexpected occasions, like sickness or mishaps, limiting the monetary effect on people and their families.

5. Home Preparation: Anticipating the dispersion of resources after death is a pivotal part of monetary preparation. In order to ensure a smooth transfer of wealth to heirs while minimizing tax liabilities, it involves the creation of wills, trusts, and other mechanisms.

6. Versatility to Life Changes: Life is dynamic, and monetary arranging obliges changes like marriage, being a parent, or profession shifts. It gives a structure to adjusting to developing conditions and changing monetary objectives in a like manner. planning and monetary arranging are basic parts of accomplishing and keeping up with monetary prosperity. While planning gives an everyday aide for overseeing pay and costs, monetary arranging adopts an all encompassing strategy, taking into account long haul objectives and methodologies for creating and protecting financial stability. Together, these practices engage people to assume command over their funds, decrease pressure, and work towards a protected and prosperous future.

Funding Options and Capital Structure

Subsidizing choices and capital construction are basic parts of an organization's monetary administration, impacting its capacity to work, develop, and endure financial difficulties. Laying out an ideal capital construction includes deciding the right blend of obligation and value funding to help the association's targets. In this investigation, we'll dig into different subsidizing choices and look at the complexities of creating a compelling capital construction.

Subsidizing Choices:

Value Funding: Value funding includes raising capital by selling possession stakes in the organization. Normal sources incorporate introductory public contributions (Initial public offerings), confidential positions, and funding speculations. It provides funds without requiring debt, but it also dilutes existing ownership and may require giving up some control to investors from outside the company.

Obligation Supporting: Debt financing involves borrowing money and repaying it over time with interest. Sources incorporate bank advances, securities, and other obligation instruments. Despite the fact that it permits organizations to keep up with possession control, unnecessary obligations can prompt monetary strain because of interest installments and the commitment to reimburse chief sums.

Bootstrapping: Bootstrapping includes depending on private reserve funds, income created by the business, and parsimonious spending to finance activities. Even though it avoids external financing, it may limit the company's growth potential, especially in industries that require a lot of capital.

Awards and Sponsorships: Government agencies, non-governmental organizations, and other organizations may offer grants or subsidies to certain businesses. These assets are frequently reserved for explicit purposes, like innovative work or maintainability drives.

Crowdfunding: Crowdfunding stages permit organizations to collect limited quantities of cash from countless people. This technique has acquired prominence, particularly for new companies and imaginative undertakings, however achievement relies upon compelling promoting and commitment with the group.

Capital Organization: Deciding Ideal Capital Design: Finding a balance between equity and debt in order to maximize the company's value and reduce its cost of capital is necessary to achieve an optimal capital structure.

These decisions are influenced by things like industry norms, risk tolerance, and growth prospects.

Cost of Capital: The total cost of debt and equity financing is the cost of capital. Offsetting cheaper obligations with greater expense value is pivotal. A lot of obligations can prompt monetary trouble, while a lot of value might bring about higher weakening and a less productive capital design.

Modigliani-Mill operator Hypothesis: The Modigliani-Mill operator hypothesis recommends that, under specific presumptions, the worth of a firm is free of its capital design. While this hypothesis gives a hypothetical system, genuine contemplations and market blemishes frequently lead organizations to structure their capital cautiously.

Influence Proportions: Influence proportions, like obligation to-value proportions, measure the extent of obligation in an organization's capital design. High influence can intensify returns yet additionally increments monetary gamble. Organizations should assess their gamble resilience and the effect of influence on benefit.

Adaptability in Capital Construction: Keeping up with adaptability in the capital design is significant, particularly in unique business conditions. Having the option to adjust to changing monetary circumstances or open doors might require a blend of present moment and long haul funding choices.

Difficulties and Contemplations:

Situation on the Market: Monetary circumstances, loan fees, and the accessibility of subsidizing in the monetary business sectors essentially influence an organization's capacity to get funding at ideal terms.

Credit Scores: A company's ability to obtain debt financing is influenced by its credit rating. Keeping major areas of strength for a profile is fundamental for arranging ideal loan fees and terms.

Business Lifecycle: A company's requirements for funding are influenced by its lifecycle stage. New businesses might depend vigorously on value support, while laid out firms might utilize a blend of obligation and value to improve their capital construction.

Conformity to Law: Regulators' capital structure requirements must be followed by businesses. For instance, regulators may impose specific capital adequacy ratios on financial institutions. creating a viable capital construction includes a nuanced comprehension of subsidizing choices, risk resilience, and market elements.

Organizations should cautiously survey their monetary necessities, consider the compromises among obligation and value, and stay versatile to evolving conditions. The transaction between subsidizing choices and capital design is an essential choice that fundamentally impacts an organization's monetary wellbeing and long haul achievement.

Chapter 7
Marketing and Branding

Showcasing and marking are two interconnected support points that assume a significant part in the outcome of any business. These ideas are frequently utilized conversely, yet they play particular parts in molding an organization's personality, drawing in clients, and cultivating long haul connections.

Marketing: Showcasing is an exhaustive procedure that includes different exercises pointed toward advancing and selling items or administrations. It incorporates statistical surveying, promoting, advertising, and deals. A definitive objective of promoting is to make mindfulness, produce interest, and drive client commitment.

Statistical surveying: Leading careful statistical surveying is the underpinning of any effective showcasing effort. This includes breaking down purchaser requirements, inclinations, and ways of behaving. By understanding the market, organizations can fit their techniques to satisfy client needs.

Advertising: Publicizing is a critical part of showcasing that includes advancing items or administrations through different channels. This can incorporate customary mediums like TV, radio, and print, as well as computerized stages like virtual entertainment, web search tools, and sites. Advertising that works well not only gets new customers but also makes the brand more visible in the market.

Relations with media: Advertising (PR) centers around overseeing and keeping a positive picture for an organization. It involves forming connections with customers, the media, and other stakeholders. A solid PR system can improve a brand's standing and believability, adding to long haul achievement.

Sales: Deals are the immediate aftereffect of compelling advertising endeavors. A professional promoting system creates leads and converts them into clients. Outreach groups assume a pivotal part in this cycle, transforming likely clients into faithful supporters.

Branding: Marking is the method involved with making a particular character for an organization, item, or administration. It goes past logos and trademarks, enveloping the general insight and profound association that clients have with a brand.

Brand Character: Laying out serious areas of strength for a character includes characterizing the basic beliefs, mission, and vision of a business. This character is passed on through components like logos, colors, and visual style, making an unmistakable and noteworthy brand picture.

Brand Situating: Brand situating is about how a brand is seen in contrast with contenders. It includes recognizing a remarkable selling recommendation (USP) that separates the brand in the personalities of customers. Compelling situating assists focus on the right crowd and fabricate a dependable client with basing.

Brand Reliability: Building brand faithfulness is pivotal for supported achievement. Customers who are devoted to a brand become advocates as well as repeat customers. Brand loyalty is cultivated through consistent quality, positive customer experiences, and efficient communication.

Brand Augmentation: Brand augmentation includes utilizing a laid out brand to present new items or administrations. When carried out successfully, it makes use of the trust and recognition that are already associated with the brand. As a result, the amount of effort required to market the new products is reduced.

Combination of Advertising and Marking: While advertising and marking are unmistakable ideas, they are intrinsically associated. Powerful showcasing systems add to building and advancing a brand, while a solid brand improves the effect of promoting endeavors.

Reliable Informing: Incorporating promoting and marketing requires reliable informing across all channels. Whether through publicizing, web-based entertainment, or client corporations, the brand's character and values ought to stay durable, building up a bound together message.

Client Experience: Both showcasing and marking mean to make positive client encounters. Showcasing draws in clients through advancements and missions, while marking guarantees that these encounters line up with the general brand personality, encouraging a feeling of trust and dependability.

Criticism Circle: A cooperative relationship exists among showcasing and marking through client input. Showcasing endeavors create bits of knowledge into buyer inclinations and ways of behaving, which, thusly, can shape and refine the brand technique to all the more likely reverberate with the interest group. promoting and marketing are basic parts of a fruitful business system.

While showcasing drives transient outcomes by advancing items and administrations, marking constructs the drawn out standing and devotion that supports a business over the long haul.

The coordination of these two components is pivotal for making a comprehensive methodology that draws in clients as well as lays out areas of strength for a getting through brand presence on the lookout.

Crafting an Effective Marketing Strategy

Making a successful promoting methodology is fundamental for organizations endeavoring to hang out in the present serious scene. The organization's objectives are aligned with market trends through a well-thought-out plan, which also aids in customer acquisition and retention. In this investigation of making a successful promoting methodology, we'll dive into key parts, contemplations, and arising patterns that can shape your methodology.

Figuring out Your Interest group: The groundwork of any fruitful showcasing procedure lies in figuring out your interest group. Demographics, preferences, and behaviors can all be identified with the help of comprehensive market research. This information permits you to tailor your informing, channels, and advancements to reverberate with your crowd. Use reviews, online entertainment examination, and client input to refine how you might interpret your ideal interest group persistently.

Having Specific Goals: Characterize quantifiable and practical targets to direct your showcasing endeavors. Whether it's rising image mindfulness, driving deals, or extending a piece of the pie, having clear objectives gives guidance and helps in assessing achievement. Utilize the Brilliant models — Explicit, Quantifiable, Reachable, Important, and Time-bound — to guarantee your goals are obvious and significant.

SWOT Examination: Direct a complete SWOT investigation to recognize Qualities, Shortcomings, Valuable open doors, and Dangers. Understanding inward qualities and shortcomings helps with utilizing or alleviating them, while perceiving outside valuable open doors and dangers takes into consideration vital preparation. Strategies that take advantage of opportunities and strengths while addressing threats and weaknesses are based on this analysis.

Separation and Extraordinary Selling Recommendation (USP): Distinguish what separates your item or administration from contenders. Making an extraordinary selling suggestion features the particular worth your contribution gives. Whether it's unrivaled quality, imaginative highlights, or extraordinary client support, a convincing USP makes an important brand personality and resonates with your interest group.

Multi-Channel Approach: To reach a larger audience, diversify your marketing channels. From customary channels like television and radio to computerized stages like web-based entertainment, email, and web crawlers, a multi-station approach guarantees that your message is passed on through different touchpoints. Choose channels that are in line with your overall marketing goals and take into consideration the preferences of your target audience.

Marketing via Content: Make important and pertinent substance to connect with your crowd. Content promoting lays out your image as an expert in your industry, fabricates trust, and draws in possible clients. Foster a substance schedule that lines up with your promoting objectives, integrating blog entries, articles, recordings, and infographics. Reliable and top notch content adds to long haul brand perceivability and client steadfastness.

Using Information and Investigation: Influence information and investigation to go with educated choices and measure the adequacy regarding your promoting endeavors.

Screen key execution markers (KPIs, for example, change rates, site traffic, and virtual entertainment commitment. Breaking down information gives experiences into shopper conduct, empowering you to refine your methodologies for improved results.

Embracing Innovation and Robotization: To simplify your marketing procedures, investigate automation tools and technological solutions. Promoting computerization stages can assist with assignments like email crusades, lead sustaining, and client division. Embracing arising advances, like man-made consciousness and increased reality, can likewise furnish inventive ways of drawing in with your crowd.

Building Connections through Online Entertainment: Engage your audience on social media to foster brand loyalty and establish relationships. Online entertainment is an integral asset for making a two-way correspondence channel with your clients. Consistently share refreshes, answer remarks, and run designated missions to keep your crowd drew in and associated with your image.

Versatility and Adaptability: The showcasing scene is dynamic, with patterns and buyer ways of behaving advancing quickly. A fruitful promoting system requires versatility and adaptability to answer changing economic situations. Routinely reconsider your procedures, remain informed about industry drifts, and change your way to deal with meeting the developing requirements of your interest group.

Estimating and Emphasizing: Consistent improvement is essential in showcasing. Routinely measure the presentation of your missions against laid out KPIs and accumulate criticism from clients. Utilize this data to repeat and improve your methodologies. You can improve the efficiency of your marketing efforts as a whole, refine your messaging, and make decisions based on accurate data with a data-driven approach.

Moral Contemplations: Ethical considerations ought to be incorporated into your marketing strategy in this time of increased awareness. Straightforwardness, validness, and socially mindful practices resound decidedly with customers. Be aware of the effect your showcasing efforts might have on society and the climate, and adjust your image to values that reverberate with your ideal interest group.

Creating a powerful showcasing methodology includes an all encompassing methodology that considers the one of a kind qualities of your business, industry patterns, and the consistently developing inclinations of your interest group. By figuring out your crowd, setting clear goals, using different channels, making convincing substance, and embracing innovation, you can construct a strong showcasing system that draws in clients as well as encourages long haul brand achievement. To ensure that your marketing efforts remain relevant and have an impact in the ever-changing business landscape, you need to be adaptable, measure performance, and iterate.

Building a Strong Brand Identity

Building areas of strength for a personality is an urgent part of laying out an effective and unmistakable presence on the lookout. A brand personality goes past a logo or a slogan; it incorporates the general insight and feelings related with a brand. In this article, we will dig into the critical parts and systems engaged with making a vigorous brand character.

1. Figuring out Your Image: Prior to setting out on the excursion of building a brand personality, having a profound comprehension of your brand is fundamental. What values does it address? What is its objective? The creation of a consistent and authentic identity will be guided by an understanding of your brand's essence.

2. Characterize Your Ideal interest group: When creating a brand identity that resonates with the right people, it is essential to identify and comprehend your target audience. Lead statistical surveying to appreciate the necessities, inclinations, and ways of behaving of your crowd. Your brand's design and messaging will be influenced by this information.

3. Foster an Extraordinary Offer: A solid brand character is based on an interesting incentive that separates your image from rivals. Obviously lucid what makes your image exceptional and why purchasers ought to pick it over others. All facets of your brand identity should incorporate this idea.

4. Plan a Noteworthy Logo: A logo is in many cases the principal visual component individuals partner with a brand. Put time and assets in making an unmistakable and essential logo that mirrors your image's character. Guarantee that it is adaptable, flexible, and effectively conspicuous across different stages and mediums.

5. Choose a Color Scheme That Stays the Same: Colors summon feelings and assume a critical part in brand discernment. Select a variety range that lines up with your image character and reverberates with your ideal interest group. Consistency in variety utilization across all brand materials encourages acknowledgment and supports brand personality.

6. Make a One of a kind Brand Voice: The language and tone utilized in your correspondence materials add to the general brand character. Foster a novel brand voice that mirrors your image's character and resounds with your crowd. Whether it's formal, fun loving, or legitimate, consistency is critical.

7. Lay out Brand Rules: To guarantee consistency across all brand touchpoints, lay out far reaching brand rules. These rules ought to cover logo use, variety plans, typography, and manner of speaking. Having a bunch of clear rules keeps a strong brand character, particularly as your image extends.

8. Fabricate a Responsive Site: In the advanced age, your site is many times the primary association clients have with your image. Make sure the design of your website matches your brand's identity to create a seamless and visually cohesive experience. Advance it for both work area and portable clients to improve openness.

9. Influence Virtual Entertainment Actually: Web-based entertainment stages are useful assets for brand advancement. Through consistent visuals, messaging, and engagement, make use of these channels to bolster your brand identity. Routinely update content and draw in with your crowd to cultivate a feeling of local area around your image.

10. Recount Your Image Story: Stories captivate customers. Make a convincing brand story that imparts your set of experiences, values, and excursion. Share this story across different channels, including your site, web-based entertainment, and showcasing materials. A very much recounted story can make a close to home connection between your image and its crowd.

11. Cultivate Brand Consistency: Consistency is the bedrock of a solid brand character. Whether it's in publicizing, bundling, client communications, or some other touchpoint, keeping up with consistency constructs trust and acknowledgment. Consistently review your image materials to guarantee they line up with laid out rules.

12. Adjust to Market Patterns: While keeping up with consistency, it's vital to stay sensitive to showcase patterns. A brand that adjusts to developing buyer inclinations and industry changes stays important. This doesn't mean a total redesign yet rather essential changes that line up with the center brand character.

13. Look for Client Criticism: Criticism from your crowd gives significant bits of knowledge into how your image is seen. Effectively look for and pay attention to client input, whether positive or negative. Utilize this data to refine your image personality, tending to any areas that may not be resounding as planned.

14. Team up with Powerhouses: Cooperating with powerhouses who line up with your image values can broaden your compass and improve validity. Forces to be reckoned with can genuinely coordinate your image into their substance, presenting it to their supporters in an engaging manner.

15. Develop with Reason: As your image develops, intermittent advancement might be vital. Notwithstanding, any progressions ought to be deliberate and line up with the guiding principle of your image. An insightful development guarantees that your image stays pertinent without losing its personality.

fabricating areas of strength for a personality is a continuous cycle that requires a profound comprehension of your image, crowd, and market elements. By decisively consolidating these components and reliably building up your image personality across all touchpoints, you can make an enduring and significant presence in the personalities of customers.

Chapter 8
Leadership and Team Building

Authority and group building are basic parts of innovative achievement. In the ever-changing and dynamic world of entrepreneurship, good leadership can make the difference between a successful and unsuccessful venture. This article investigates the entwined ideas of authority and group working with regards to business, featuring key standards and procedures for encouraging a culture of development, cooperation, and supported development.

Authority in Business: At the center of effective business venture is visionary initiative. Entrepreneurs frequently have to overcome obstacles, make difficult choices, and motivate their teams to achieve lofty objectives. A solid innovative pioneer has a blend of vital reasoning, versatility, and strength.

Vision and Mission: Business people should express a convincing vision and mission for their endeavors. This gives a reasonable course and motivation, adjusting the group towards shared objectives. An obvious vision fills in as a directing light, assisting the group with exploring difficulties and keeping fixed on long haul goals.

Adaptability: The innovative excursion is laden with vulnerabilities and surprising difficulties. Compelling pioneers show flexibility, embracing change and transforming deterrents into open doors. This adaptability is essential in a unique business climate where quick changes might be important for endurance and development.

Risk-Taking and Development: Pioneering pioneers are intrinsically daring people. They support a culture of well balanced plan of action taking inside the group, encouraging development and imagination. By embracing trial and error and gaining from disappointments, pioneers establish a climate where momentous thoughts can thrive.

Decision-Making: Fast and informed direction is a sign of compelling enterprising initiative. Pioneers should gauge the advantages and disadvantages quickly, taking into account the possible effect on the business. Definitiveness imparts trust in the group and forestalls loss of motion by examination, empowering the association to remain lithe.

Group Working in Business venture: For the success of an entrepreneur, it is equally important to form a team that works well together. A well-working group can conquer difficulties, adjust to change, and drive development. Here are key parts of a group working in a business venture:

Variety and Incorporation: A different group offers shifted viewpoints and abilities that would be useful.

Incorporation guarantees that each colleague feels esteemed, cultivating a cooperative climate. Embracing variety in the entirety of its structures advances imagination and assists the group with exploring complex issues all the more really.

Communication: Viable correspondence is the bedrock of effective groups. Business people should lay out open and straightforward correspondence channels. Normal group gatherings, criticism meetings, and clear documentation of objectives and assumptions add to a common perspective of the organization's vision and individual jobs.

Trust and Responsibility: Trust is the underpinning areas of strength for elements. Business visionaries should develop a culture of trust by being straightforward, solid, and steady. Furthermore, cultivating a feeling of responsibility guarantees that colleagues take responsibility for obligations, advancing an outcomes situated mentality.

Empowerment: Effective business people enable their groups by giving independence and open doors to proficient development. Team members are more likely to take the lead, come up with novel ideas, and anticipate problems when they have a sense of authority and trust.

Solution of Conflicts: Clashes are unavoidable in any group setting. Business people should foster compelling compromise abilities to resolve issues immediately and productively. Taking care of contentions with awareness and decency reinforces group union and forestalls waiting hatred.

Incorporating Authority and Group Building: Entrepreneurship truly thrives when leadership and team building work together. Here are techniques to flawlessly incorporate these components: Show others how it's done: Successful pioneers set the vibe for the group by exemplifying the qualities and hard working attitude they anticipate. Showing others how it's done cultivates a positive culture where difficult work, trustworthiness, and responsibility are the standard.

Encourage a Culture of Learning: Enterprising pioneers ought to empower a persistent learning outlook inside the group. This includes putting resources into proficient improvement open doors, sharing information, and establishing a climate where slip-ups are viewed as learning open doors.

Recognize accomplishments: Perceiving and commending accomplishments, both of all shapes and sizes, lifts group feelings of confidence and inspiration. Business visionaries ought to find an opportunity to recognize and compensate for the difficult work and achievements of their colleagues.

Criticism Circle: For advancement, a robust feedback loop must be established. It is possible to discuss performance, pinpoint areas for improvement, and address concerns during regular feedback sessions. Useful criticism cultivates a culture of constant improvement.

Empower Cooperation: Innovative pioneers ought to effectively advance cooperation among colleagues. Cross-useful coordinated effort supports the trading of thoughts and abilities, driving advancement and critical thinking. end: administration and group building are entwined mainstays of progress in business.

Visionary pioneers who focus on compelling correspondence, encourage a positive group culture, and show others how it's done establish a climate where groups flourish and organizations thrive. By embracing variety, advancing a learning society, and incorporating criticism circles, business visionaries can construct versatile groups equipped for exploring the difficulties of the enterprising excursion. In the high speed universe of business, the capacity to motivate and join a group towards a typical vision is a characterizing factor that isolates the effective endeavors from the rest.

Effective Leadership Qualities

Compelling authority in business ventures is urgent for controlling an organization towards progress. A gifted business visionary recognizes open doors as well as has key characteristics that rouse and direct a group. These characteristics are fundamental in encouraging development, versatility, and a positive working environment culture.

One central attribute of compelling pioneering administration is vision. An effective business person has a reasonable vision of the organization's future and can verbalize it to the group. This clearness gives guidance, adjusting the endeavors of each and every colleague towards shared objectives. An obvious vision likewise helps in settling on essential choices and exploring difficulties, as it fills in as a directing light during unsure times. Another fundamental quality is flexibility.

The business scene is dynamic, and a successful business person should be adaptable in light of evolving conditions. Versatile pioneers can turn their methodologies, embrace new advances, and change their methodologies in view of market patterns. This flexibility is essential in supporting and growing a business in a consistently developing climate. Relational abilities are vital for pioneering pioneers.

A productive and healthy work environment is created when people are able to clearly communicate their ideas, actively listen, and offer constructive feedback. Compelling correspondence guarantees that everybody in the group figures out the vision, mission, and objectives, decreasing the probability of false impressions and advancing a strong group dynamic. The fact that sets fruitful business visionaries separate makes, besides, adaptability a key characteristic.

The enterprising excursion is filled with obstructions and misfortunes. When confronted with difficulties, a resilient leader maintains a positive outlook and recovers from setbacks. This resilience inspires the team to persevere and overcome adversity as well as the leader. Compassion is one more basic quality for compelling authority in business. Grasping the necessities, concerns, and inspirations of colleagues cultivates a steady and comprehensive workplace.

A compassionate pioneer esteems the prosperity of the group, advances balance between serious and fun activities, and perceives the remarkable qualities every individual offers that would be useful. Conclusiveness is an imperative quality in the quick moving universe of business. Leaders must make decisions promptly and based on information, frequently with incomplete data. Leaders who are decisive look at the risks, collect relevant data, and make choices that are in line with the goals of the company.

Uncertainty can prompt botched open doors, deferred progress, and an absence of certainty among colleagues. Notwithstanding definitiveness, a compelling appointment is vital. Business visionaries can't do everything all alone, and entrusting the group with liabilities is an indication of a solid chief. Designating assignments in light of colleagues' assets engages the group as well as permits the pioneer to zero in on essential parts of the business. A pledge to constant learning is a sign of compelling pioneering initiative.

Leaders need to keep up with industry trends, emerging technologies, and best practices because the business landscape is always changing. A pledge to learning upgrades the pioneer's information as well as sets a model for the group, empowering a culture of persistent improvement. Key reasoning is a quality that empowers business visionaries to anticipate the future and expect market patterns. Powerful pioneers evaluate the serious scene, recognize open doors for development, and figure out long haul systems.

Vital reasoning remains inseparable with the capacity to focus on assignments, guaranteeing that the group centers around drives that line up with the general vision and objectives.

successful administration in business ventures requires a mix of vision, versatility, relational abilities, strength, sympathy, definitiveness, designation, a guarantee to ceaseless learning, and key reasoning. These characteristics not only improve the leader's ability to overcome obstacles but also contribute to the company's overall success and sustainability. Business people who encapsulate these initiative characteristics are better prepared to rouse their groups, encourage development, and make long haul progress in a cutthroat business climate.

Fostering a Positive and Productive Team Culture

It is essential to the success of an entrepreneur to cultivate a team culture that is constructive and productive. In the dynamic and serious scene of business, a durable and persuaded group can be the main impetus behind development, imagination, and eventually, business development. This article investigates key procedures and standards to develop a positive and useful group culture inside a pioneering setting.

1. Clear Correspondence: A positive team culture is built on strong communication. Business people should lay out straightforward channels of correspondence to guarantee that data streams openly among colleagues. Customary group gatherings, open discussions, and clear documentation of objectives and assumptions add to a mutual perspective of the organization's vision and mission.

2. Shared Vision and Values: A pioneering group ought to adjust around a common vision and guiding principle. At the point when colleagues all in all embrace a typical reason, it encourages a feeling of having a place and solidarity. Laying out areas of strength for any of values supports the ideal culture and helps guide dynamic cycles inside the group.

3. Strengthening and Independence: Empowering colleagues to take responsibility for work and giving them a feeling of independence can fundamentally upgrade efficiency and occupation fulfillment. Business people ought to engage their group by confiding in their capacities and giving them the opportunity to settle on choices inside their particular jobs.

4. Acknowledgment and Appreciation: Recognizing and valuing the endeavors of colleagues is indispensable for keeping up with spirit. Business people ought to effectively perceive individual and aggregate accomplishments, building up a positive climate and spurring colleagues to succeed in their obligations.

5. Create a Culture of Learning: In the quickly developing enterprising scene, a culture of ceaseless learning is fundamental. Business visionaries ought to set out open doors for expertise advancement, preparing projects, and information sharing inside the group. This improves individual capacities as well as adds to the general development of the association.

6. Comprehensive and Different Climate: Variety in the group, both concerning foundations and points of view, can prompt more extravagant critical thinking and creative thoughts. Business visionaries ought to effectively advance a comprehensive climate where all colleagues feel esteemed and regarded, independent of their disparities.

7. Adaptability and Flexibility: The innovative excursion is frequently set apart by vulnerabilities and fast changes. A positive group culture embraces adaptability and versatility. Colleagues ought to be urged to embrace change, gain from difficulties, and adjust their systems to advancing conditions.

8. Empower Joint effort: It is essential for team members to work together to accomplish common objectives. Business visionaries ought to cultivate a cooperative soul by giving instruments and stages that work with collaboration. Group building exercises, both inside and outside the working environment, can likewise add to more grounded bonds among colleagues.

9. Adjusting Work and Prosperity: Work-life balance and well-being are crucial for entrepreneurs. A positive group culture esteems the wellbeing and bliss of its individuals. Adaptable work game plans, psychological wellness backing, and drives that advance a solid way of life add to a more feasible and useful workplace.

10. Show others how its done: Enterprising pioneers assume a crucial part in molding the group culture. The team's tone is set by leading by example, exhibiting the desired values, and maintaining a positive attitude. Entrepreneurs should show their team that they are dedicated, passionate, and resilient by actively engaging with them.

cultivating a positive and useful group culture in a pioneering setting requires a purposeful and continuous exertion. Clear correspondence, shared vision, strengthening, acknowledgment, and a guarantee to learning are fundamental components. Innovation, employee satisfaction, and ultimately business success are more likely to come from entrepreneurs who place a strong emphasis on team culture.

Chapter 9
Scaling the Business

Scaling a business is a diverse undertaking that includes extending tasks, expanding income streams, and adjusting to a developing business sector. Fruitful scaling requires key preparation, powerful execution, and a sharp comprehension of the market elements. In this investigation of scaling a business, we'll dig into key contemplations, difficulties, and systems that business visionaries and business pioneers ought to remember.

1. **Grasping Scaling:** Scaling a business goes past simply expanding its size. It includes a deliberate and practical development that permits the organization to effectively deal with development. This can be accomplished in a number of ways, including expanding the customer base, entering new markets, diversifying product and service offerings, and increasing production capacity.

2. **Vital Preparation:** Viable scaling begins with powerful essential preparation. Organizations need to characterize their drawn out objectives, survey market amazing open doors, and recognize expected difficulties. A thorough field-tested strategy ought to frame the means expected for development, including monetary

projections, asset distribution, and hazard the executives procedures.

3. **Financial acuity:** Monetary soundness is urgent for scaling. Organizations need to assess their monetary wellbeing, guaranteeing that they have the essential money to help development. This might include getting extra subsidizing through credits, financial backers, or associations. Judicious monetary administration is fundamental to keep away from overleveraging and keep a sound income.

4. **Functional Effectiveness:** Scaling requests expanded functional proficiency. To handle higher volumes, businesses should streamline procedures, make use of technology, and implement scalable systems. Computerization can assume a vital part in lessening manual undertakings, limiting blunders, and working on general productivity.

5. **Recruiting and Developing People:** A workforce that is skilled and enthusiastic is necessary for a growing business. Scaling requires vital ability obtaining and improvement drives. This incorporates employing the perfect individuals, giving preparation, and cultivating a positive work culture that empowers development and coordinated effort.

6. **Client Obtaining and Maintenance:** Extending the client base is a crucial part of scaling. In order to reach new customers and maintain existing ones, businesses must prioritize marketing strategies that work. Building solid associations with existing clients

can prompt recurrent business and positive verbal exchange references.

7. Statistical surveying and Variation: For successful scaling, it is essential to comprehend the market. Persistent statistical surveying assists organizations with remaining informed about industry patterns, client inclinations, and cutthroat scenes. It is essential for sustained growth to be adaptable and willing to pivot in response to feedback from the market.

8. Versatile Innovation Foundation: To meet rising demands, a technology infrastructure that can grow with the business is essential. This includes updating programming, taking on cloud-based arrangements, and guaranteeing that the IT foundation can flawlessly oblige development without compromising execution or security.

9. Risk The board: Scaling implies innate dangers, and organizations should have a powerful gamble the executives methodology set up. This incorporates recognizing possible difficulties, creating emergency courses of action, and having a proactive way to deal with and address unexpected issues.

10. Associations and Coordinated efforts: Vital organizations and joint efforts can speed up the scaling system. Shaping coalitions with different organizations, providers, or wholesalers can give admittance to new business sectors, assets, and ability.

Challenges in Scaling: In spite of the expected advantages, scaling a business isn't without challenges. Management of increased complexity, upholding quality standards, and ensuring that the organization's culture endures growth are all common obstacles. Monetary limitations and market vulnerabilities can likewise present huge difficulties.

Procedures for Beating Difficulties: Tending to these difficulties requires a proactive methodology. Organizations ought to focus on powerful correspondence, put resources into worker preparing, and stay dexterous in their dynamic cycles. In addition, seeking advice from mentors, industry professionals, or advisory boards can offer useful insights.

Scaling a business is a dynamic process that requires flexibility, careful planning, and execution. By zeroing in on essential preparation, monetary readiness, functional effectiveness, and other key elements, organizations can situate themselves for feasible development. Embracing difficulties as any open doors for learning and improvement is fundamental for exploring the intricacies of scaling and making long haul progress.

Strategies for Growth and Expansion

In the unique scene of business, development and extension are frequently basic for long haul achievement. Whether a little startup or a laid out enterprise, associations look for methodologies to scale their tasks, increment a portion of the overall industry, and remain in front of the opposition. The various growth and expansion strategies discussed in this essay take into account both internal and external factors that can affect an organization's trajectory.

1. Market Entrance: Market penetration is one fundamental growth strategy. Utilizing the products or services that are already available, this entails expanding one's share of the market in existing markets. Organizations frequently accomplish this through forceful advertising, evaluating systems, or upgrading circulation channels. A business might, for instance, start loyalty programs to keep its current clients happy and attract new ones, thereby securing its position in the market.

2. Item Improvement: Presenting new items or further developing existing ones is one more road for development. Organizations put resources into innovative work to develop and meet changing client needs This methodology requires a profound comprehension of customer inclinations and market patterns. Apple, for instance, reliably dispatches new renditions of its items, gaining by mechanical headways and shopper interest for the most recent elements.

3. Market Improvement: Venturing into new business sectors geologically or demographically is a system known as market improvement. This could include focusing on various client fragments, entering worldwide business sectors, or expanding into districts with undiscovered capacity. Mcdonald's, for example, adjusts its menu to suit neighborhood tastes while entering new global business sectors, growing its client base.

4. Diversification: Broadening includes entering new business sectors with new items or administrations. This methodology can be unsafe yet can likewise prompt significant prizes. Organizations might choose related broadening, where new items or administrations supplement existing ones, or irrelevant enhancement, wandering into totally various ventures. Aggregates like General Electric embody irrelevant enhancement, working in areas as different as aeronautics, medical care, and energy.

5. Key Collusions and Organizations: One important growth strategy is collaboration through strategic alliances or partnerships. By uniting with different associations, organizations can get to new business sectors, advances, or conveyance channels. Joint endeavors and key organizations permit organizations to share dangers and assets. For instance, the Nike+iPod sports kit was the result of a partnership between Nike and Apple that combined their expertise in technology and sportswear to produce a product that was beneficial to both parties.

6. Consolidations and Acquisitions: Consolidations and acquisitions (M&A) are vital moves that include joining or buying different organizations. M&A can give fast development, cooperative energies, and cost efficiencies. However, thorough due diligence and integration planning are necessary for successful execution.

A model is Facebook's procurement of Instagram, which killed an expected contender as well as enhanced Facebook's virtual entertainment environment.

7. Franchising: Diversifying is a powerful procedure for extension, especially for organizations with an effective and replicable model. Franchisees receive licenses from franchisors to use the established brand and business model in their locations. This permits the franchisor to grow quickly with lower capital ventures. Starbucks, McDonald's, and Subway are just a few examples of globally successful franchises.

8. Internet business and Computerized Change: In the computerized age, utilizing innovation is fundamental for development. Online business and advanced change can open new roads for organizations. Organizations can contact a worldwide crowd, upgrade tasks, and improve client encounters through web-based stages. Amazon's development from a web-based book shop to a worldwide online business monster shows the extraordinary force of computerized procedures for development.

9. Client Maintenance and Faithfulness Projects: While gaining new clients is critical, it is similarly vital to hold existing ones. Executing client maintenance procedures and devotion projects can upgrade consumer loyalty and fabricate long haul connections. Loyalty programs have been used successfully by Starbucks and Amazon Prime to create a sense of exclusivity among their customers and encourage repeat business.

10. Nonstop Advancement: A culture of constant development is fundamental for supported development. Organizations that focus on development stay ahead in the market by adjusting to changing patterns and client inclinations. Tesla, with its emphasis on electric vehicles and sustainable power arrangements, represents how advancement can disturb conventional ventures and drive development.

Procedures for development and extension are multi-layered, requiring a nuanced comprehension of market elements, client conduct, and serious scenes. Associations should cautiously assess their assets, shortcomings, open doors, and dangers to plan compelling development procedures. Whether through market infiltration, item improvement, unions, or computerized change, the quest for development requests key vision, flexibility, and a guarantee to convey worth to clients.

In a steadily advancing business climate, the capacity to explore these techniques handily can decide the achievement and life span of an association.

Managing Scale-Related Challenges

Managing difficulties related to scale is an essential part of entrepreneurship, particularly as a company grows. Scaling a business carries with it an extraordinary arrangement of chances and deterrents that require key reasoning and versatility. In this conversation, we will dive into different parts of overseeing scale-related difficulties in business ventures, investigating the key regions where organizations frequently experience hardships and offering bits of knowledge into powerful arrangements.

1. Monetary Administration: One of the essential difficulties while scaling a business is guaranteeing legitimate monetary administration. As tasks develop, costs will quite often increment, and it becomes essential to keep a harmony between income age and cost control. Business visionaries should foster vigorous monetary frameworks, screen income carefully, and make vital speculations to maintain and upgrade development.

2. Ability Securing and Maintenance: Scaling a business frequently requires extending the group to fulfill the developing needs. Notwithstanding, finding and holding top ability can be a huge test. Business people should zero in on building areas of strength for a culture, offering cutthroat pay bundles, and giving open doors to proficient improvement to draw in and hold talented representatives.

3. Functional Effectiveness: The operational complexity of a business grows with it. Business people should persistently survey and advance cycles to guarantee productivity. Carrying out versatile advances, computerizing routine undertakings, and encouraging a culture of development can assist with smoothing out tasks and improve by and large effectiveness.

4. Consumer loyalty: Maintaining high levels of customer satisfaction becomes more difficult as the customer base grows. Business people need to put resources into the client assistance framework, assemble criticism, and use information examination to comprehend client needs. Building solid associations with clients is fundamental for supporting development.

5. Versatile Innovation Framework: For handling increased workloads and maintaining performance, a technology infrastructure that is scalable is essential. Taking into account factors like data security, system dependability, and the capacity to adapt to changing business requirements, entrepreneurs must invest in IT systems that are both robust and scalable.

6. Market Growth: Scaling frequently includes entering new business sectors, which presents its own arrangement of difficulties. Business visionaries should lead careful statistical surveying, adjust promoting procedures to nearby inclinations, and explore administrative scenes. A thoroughly examined market extension plan is fundamental for maintainable development.

7. Production network The executives: With expanded request, production network the executives turns out to be more perplexing. Business visionaries need to lay areas of strength out with providers, upgrade stock levels, and execute effective strategies to guarantee a smooth production network that can uphold development without compromising quality.

8. Conformity to Law: A wider range of laws and regulations apply to a growing business. To navigate complex regulatory landscapes, entrepreneurs need to stay informed about the legal requirements in various jurisdictions, implement compliance measures, and have a strong legal team. The business could face serious consequences if it does not comply.

9. Brand The board: Keeping a steady and positive brand picture becomes testing as a business scales. In order to ensure that the brand message is in line with the company's values and reaches a wide range of customers, entrepreneurs must invest in brand management strategies.

10. Risk The executives: With development comes expanded openness to different dangers. Business people must proactively distinguish and evaluate likely dangers, foster gamble moderation techniques, and have emergency courses of action set up. This includes risks to the business's finances, the market, and its operations.

overseeing scale-related difficulties in business requires a complete and versatile methodology. Business people should be proactive in tending to monetary, functional, ability, and administrative difficulties. Building a versatile and proficient plan of action, cultivating a positive organizational culture, and remaining light-footed because of market elements are key components in effectively exploring the intricacies of scaling a business. By tending to these difficulties decisively, business visionaries can accomplish economical development as well as position their endeavors for long haul outcome in a serious business scene.

Chapter 10
Case Studies of Successful Entrepreneurs

Business is an excursion loaded up with difficulties, dangers, and vulnerabilities. Notwithstanding, a few people explore this way with extraordinary expertise, transforming their endeavors into striking examples of overcoming adversity. Analyzing contextual analyses of these effective business people offers important experiences into the attributes, procedures, and choices that add to their accomplishments. In this investigation, we will dig into the narratives of three different business people: Elon Musk, Oprah Winfrey, and Jack Mama.

Elon Musk, the visionary organizer behind Tesla and SpaceX, embodies tireless assurance and advancement. Brought into the world in South Africa, Musk showed an early interest in innovation and business ventures. Musk went on to co-found Zip2, a newspaper city guide software company, and founded X.com, an online payment company that was later merged into

PayPal. PayPal's prosperity furnished Musk with the monetary means to seek after his more terrific dreams.

Tesla, Musk's electric vehicle and clean energy organization, has reformed the auto business. Notwithstanding confronting doubt and monetary difficulties, Musk's resolute obligation to manageability and mechanical headway has moved Tesla to turn into a key part on the lookout. Furthermore, SpaceX, Musk's aviation organization, has accomplished achievements like reusable rocket innovation, fundamentally lessening the expense of room investigation.

Oprah Winfrey, a news big shot and humanitarian, rose up out of a provoking youth to become perhaps one of the most compelling figures in media outlets. Winfrey's career started as a commentator, however it was her job as the host of "The Oprah Winfrey Show" that shot her to fame. Her capacity to interface with crowds and examine many points added to the show's massive achievement.

Past TV, Winfrey differentiated her endeavors, including establishing Harpo Creations, delivering movies, and sending off the Oprah Winfrey Organization (OWN). Her genuineness, sympathy, and obligation to positive substance have cemented her as a social symbol. Winfrey's prosperity outlines the force of individual marking, flexibility, and a certified association with one's crowd.

Jack Mama, the pioneer behind Alibaba Gathering, is an unmistakable figure in the worldwide web based business and innovation scene. Ma's career as an entrepreneur began in China, where she worked as an English teacher. Perceiving the undiscovered possibility of the web, he established Alibaba in 1999, at first as a web-based commercial center interfacing Chinese producers with worldwide purchasers.

Alibaba's development into a far reaching web based business biological system, including stages like Taobao and Tmall, assumed a crucial part in changing China's computerized economy. As Alibaba expanded into cloud computing, digital payments (Alipay), and artificial intelligence, Ma's strategic vision extended beyond e-commerce. Alibaba's status as a global tech giant is a result of Ma's leadership style, which is characterized by taking risks and being resilient. Resilience, creativity, adaptability, and a willingness to take calculated risks are all traits that successful entrepreneurs share, as shown by these case studies.

Elon Musk's capacity to disturb conventional ventures through notable innovation, Oprah Winfrey's authority of individual marking and association, and Jack Mama's vision for the advanced future exhibit the assorted ways to enterprising achievement. Moreover, these business visionaries exhibit the significance of gaining from disappointments. Winfrey overcame a difficult upbringing, Musk overcame financial difficulties and skepticism, and Ma dealt with the complexities of China's evolving digital landscape.

Every difficulty filled in as a venturing stone, supporting that disappointments are open doors for development and learning. Fruitful business people likewise underline the meaning of major areas of strength for a successful initiative. Winfrey builds a supportive network, Ma empowers employees to contribute to Alibaba's success, and Musk executes his ambitious projects with the help of brilliant minds. Building and driving a gifted group is a basic part of maintaining and scaling a fruitful endeavor.

concentrating on the contextual analyses of effective business people gives significant experiences to hopeful business pioneers. Elon Musk, Oprah Winfrey, and Jack Mama embody assorted ways to progress, exhibiting the significance of versatility, advancement, flexibility, and powerful administration. Their accounts rouse and illuminate, filling in as reference points for those exploring the difficult yet remunerating excursion of business.

Examining Real-world Examples

Business is a unique power that impels people to transform thoughts into feasible organizations, exploring difficulties, and immediately jumping all over chances. Analyzing certifiable models gives important bits of knowledge into the different ways business visionaries take, the obstructions they survive, and the effect they make on economies and social orders.

One model business visionary is Elon Musk, known for establishing and driving various noteworthy organizations, including Tesla, SpaceX, and Neuralink. Musk's endeavors feature a mix of development, risk-taking, and a constant quest for aggressive objectives. Tesla, for example, upset the car business by advocating electric vehicles and environmentally friendly power arrangements. Musk's capacity to imagine and execute such extraordinary thoughts features the embodiment of business - distinguishing holes on the lookout and tending to them with earth shattering arrangements.

Another convincing model is the ascent of Airbnb and its originators, Brian Chesky, Nathan Blecharczyk, and Joe Gebbia. By connecting travelers to unique, local accommodations, Airbnb revolutionized the hospitality industry. The originators began by leasing pneumatic beds in their loft, exhibiting the force of genius and versatility. Airbnb's prosperity highlights the significance of perceiving undiscovered market potential and adjusting to advancing shopper inclinations.

In the tech domain, the narrative of Imprint Zuckerberg and Facebook is symbolic of enterprising achievement. From a college project, Facebook has grown into a global social media powerhouse. Zuckerberg's process mirrors the meaning of distinguishing cultural necessities and utilizing innovation to make stages that associate individuals. The impact that Facebook has had on social interaction and communication exemplifies how entrepreneurial endeavors have the power to reshape the fabric of human connectivity.

The design business additionally offers convincing innovative accounts, with figures like Coco Chanel making a permanent imprint. Chanel's imaginative plans and business sharpness changed the design scene. Her story stresses the job of imagination, strength, and a sharp comprehension of purchaser wants in building a fruitful brand. Chanel's inheritance perseveres as a demonstration of the getting through impact of innovative visionaries.

Zooming into the domain of maintainable business, Patagonia and its organizer, Yvon Chouinard, represent a guarantee to ecological stewardship. Patagonia has not just flourished as an effective outside clothing organization however has likewise turned into a boss of eco-accommodating practices. Chouinard's accentuation on corporate obligation and manageability features the potential for business to be a power for positive change.

The story of Alibaba and its founder, Jack Ma, on a different continent provides a glimpse into the transformative power of e-commerce. Alibaba arose as a prevailing player in the Chinese market and then some, displaying the potential for business to rise above borders. Jack Mama's strength and capacity to explore complex business scenes underline the significance of versatility and a worldwide viewpoint in business ventures.

In the medical care area, Elizabeth Holmes, the organizer behind Theranos, gives a wake up call. Holmes intended to change blood testing however confronted charges of extortion and moral unfortunate behavior. This model highlights the significance of moral contemplations, straightforwardness, and responsibility in business. Holmes' ruin fills in as an update that achievement based on misdirection is unreasonable.

Looking at these different pioneering stories uncovers ongoing themes and examples. Vision, flexibility, strength, and a profound comprehension of market elements are repeating topics. The capacity to recognize open doors, proceed with carefully thought out plans of action, and develop recognizes effective business visionaries from the rest. Moreover, the significance of moral contemplations couldn't possibly be more significant, as trust and respectability are basic to long haul achievement.

examining real-world entrepreneurial examples reveals a diverse array of paths individuals take to establish successful businesses in a rich narrative tapestry. Whether upsetting businesses, encouraging manageability, or reshaping cultural standards, business visionaries assume a significant part in molding what's to come. The examples gathered from these accounts act as guides for trying business people, delineating the characteristics and rules that support extraordinary progress in the unique universe of business.

Extracting Lessons and Insights

Being an entrepreneur is a dynamic journey that necessitates perseverance, inventiveness, and adaptability. A road map for aspirant business leaders can be gleaned by analyzing the experiences of successful entrepreneurs for useful lessons and insights.

These lessons cover a wide range of entrepreneurship topics, from coming up with an idea to growing a business, and they shed light on the mindset and strategies that lead to success. One principal illustration is the significance of distinguishing a real issue or need on the lookout. Effective business visionaries frequently start by tending to a trouble spot, offering an answer that reverberates with likely clients.

Understanding the client's point of view is pivotal, and this client driven approach can direct item improvement and promote systems. Besides, the capacity to embrace disappointment is a typical subject among achieved business visionaries. Disappointment is a stepping stone toward progress, not the end.Before reaching significant milestones, numerous well-known entrepreneurs encountered difficulties and setbacks. The entrepreneurial spirit is characterized by adapting strategies, learning from mistakes, and persisting in the face of adversity.

Viable correspondence is another basic example business people advance en route. Communication abilities are essential for achieving business goals, whether presenting ideas to investors, negotiating deals, or building a team. Clear and convincing correspondence encourages trust, draws in financial backers, and develops a positive hierarchical culture. Key reasoning and the capacity to turn are imperative characteristics for business people exploring the eccentric business scene.

Continuous analysis of market trends, competition, and consumer behavior by successful entrepreneurs Being available to adjusting plans of action in light of these evaluations empowers business visionaries to remain significant and immediately take advantage of arising chances.

Monetary keenness is the foundation of business ventures. Business visionaries should be proficient at overseeing spending plans, determining monetary results, and settling on informed conclusions about asset designation. Sound monetary administration guarantees the manageability and development of a business. Building major areas of strength for a propelled group is a repetitive topic in the pioneering venture. Business visionaries perceive the meaning of encircling themselves with capable people who supplement their abilities.

Employee empowerment, a culture of innovation, and a positive work environment all contribute to long-term success. Systems administration and relationship-building are necessary parts of business. Fruitful business people influence their organizations to acquire significant bits of knowledge, access assets, and structure key associations.

Mentors, peers, and industry leaders can guide you through difficult times and open doors to opportunities if you cultivate and maintain relationships with them.

Entrepreneurship depends on new ideas. Business people endeavor to make interesting offers that put their items or administrations aside. Remaining on the ball requires a pledge to nonstop getting the hang of, remaining informed about industry patterns, and cultivating a culture that energizes innovative reasoning. Sticking to moral strategic approaches is non-debatable for supportable business. Keeping up with respectability constructs entrust with clients, accomplices, and financial backers.

Moral contemplations stretch out to regions, for example, ecological manageability, fair work rehearses, and straightforward business tasks. Versatility is a vital thought for business people going for the gold achievement. Fruitful business visionaries plan their organizations in light of adaptabllily, expecting future development and arranging foundations in a like manner. This essential methodology permits organizations to adjust to changing requests and exploit development potential open doors. It is common to undervalue the importance of stress management and work-life balance for entrepreneurial well-being. The requesting idea of business expects people to focus on taking care of oneself, delegate assignments really, and develop versatility to explore the unavoidable difficulties.

removing illustrations and bits of knowledge from the encounters of effective business visionaries gives priceless direction to those setting out on their pioneering venture. The multifaceted nature of entrepreneurship necessitates a comprehensive strategy for everything from determining the requirements of the market to accepting failure, forming productive teams, and prioritizing ethical practices. Hopeful business visionaries can draw motivation from these illustrations, adjust them to their extraordinary conditions, and diagram a course toward building effective and supportable endeavors.

CONCLUSION

Key Principles and Encouragement for Aspiring Entrepreneurs

hopeful business people can explore the difficult scene of business with a solid groundwork based on key standards and support. Progress in business venture isn't exclusively about having a pivotal thought or immaculate execution; it likewise includes epitomizing specific rules that add to long haul suitability and self-awareness.

One central standard is flexibility. The path to becoming an entrepreneur is fraught with setbacks, failures, and unforeseen difficulties. Embracing disappointment as a venturing stone to progress and keeping up with flexibility notwithstanding misfortune is pivotal. Obstacles should be viewed as opportunities to learn and iterate rather than obstacles that cannot be overcome. Another foundation guideline is flexibility. In the unique business world, change is steady. Business people should be adroit at adjusting to advertise shifts, innovative headways, and advancing shopper inclinations.

Adaptability in procedure and an eagerness to turn when important can be the distinction among stagnation and reasonable development. In addition, moral contemplations ought to support each pioneering try. Building a business with respectability and a promise to moral practices encourages trust among partners, including clients, representatives, and financial backers. Transparency, honesty, and social responsibility are the foundations upon which long-term success is built. In the domain of consolation, a steady local area assumes a significant part.

Hopeful business visionaries ought to look for mentorship, organizing valuable open doors, and coordinated efforts that can give direction and encourage a feeling of having a place. During trying times, it can be helpful to surround oneself with like-minded people who have goals that are similar to one's own to gain insight and emotional support. Besides, consistent learning is an indispensable component of pioneering achievement.

The business scene is steadily developing, and remaining informed about industry patterns, arising advances, and best practices is fundamental. Entrepreneurs should adopt a growth mindset and make a lifelong commitment to learning, which encourages creativity and adaptability. Monetary education is one more vital part of consolation for yearning business people.

Understanding planning, monetary determining, and venture techniques is fundamental for economical business activities. Business visionaries ought to focus on monetary instruction to go with educated choices and explore the intricacies regarding overseeing funds actually. Embracing disappointment as a venturing stone to progress and keeping up with versatility despite difficulty is vital. Throughout the entrepreneurial journey, celebrating small victories is equally important.

Recognizing progress, regardless of how steady, lifts the general mood and energizes a positive mentality. Business people ought to carve out opportunities to ponder accomplishments, both of all shapes and sizes, to build up inspiration and certainty. As far as initiative, powerful relational abilities are essential. Clear correspondence cultivates a durable group and guarantees arrangement with the organization's vision. Business people ought to develop the capacity to convey thoughts compactly, listen effectively, and give productive criticism to construct a cooperative and propelled labor force.

Lastly, entrepreneurs need to be able to prioritize and manage their time effectively. Adjusting different parts of business, from item advancement to showcasing and client relations, requires productive allotment of time and assets. Business people ought to take on methodologies, for example, objective setting, designation, and time obstructing to upgrade efficiency and keep a sound balance between fun and serious activities.

hopeful business people setting out on the excursion of building their endeavors can benefit hugely from embracing key standards and looking for support. Versatility, flexibility, moral practices, and a guarantee to constant learning structure the bedrock of a fruitful enterprising outlook. An entrepreneur's holistic development is also aided by cultivating a supportive community, recognizing accomplishments, perfecting effective communication skills, and mastering time management. By assimilating these standards and looking for support en route, hopeful business visionaries can explore difficulties with certainly and increment their possibilities building flourishing and maintainable organizations.

www.ingramcontent.com/pod-product-compliance
Lightning Source LLC
Chambersburg PA
CBHW050307230526
45471CB00005B/2060